Advanced Word Processing®

with

Microsoft® Word

ICDL Professional®

Conor Jordan

Conor Jordan

This edition published 2022

Copyright © Conor Jordan 2022

Email: conorjordan@gmail.com

Web: www.digidiscover.com

ISBN : 978-1-7396547-8-8

International Computer Driving License, ICDL, are all registered Trademarks of ICDL Foundation Limited. The content of this book was created with permission from The ICDL Foundation Ltd.

Microsoft®, Windows®, Word®, Excel®, PowerPoint®, Access® and Outlook® are trademarks of the Microsoft Corporation. Screenshots and names were used with permission from Microsoft.

Conor Jordan is unaffiliated with Microsoft or ICDL Foundation Ltd.

The intent of this manual is to provide a guide for readers to help them understand the advanced word processing and the features associated with using Microsoft Word®.

Conor Jordan does not guarantee that readers will pass their respective exams because of reading this book. Its purpose is to enable readers to better understand the applications that may or may not help them achieve their desired results in exams.

Revision sections are for practice purposes only and are not official ICDL tests. Sample tests for each module can be downloaded from the ICDL website to prepare students for their exams.

This book aims to give readers a clear understanding of the advanced features of Microsoft Word. It aims to achieve this by providing a step-by-step guide describing the skills needed to use this application effectively.

Downloading Resources

Resources associated with this book provide the opportunity to practice the techniques outlined. This will save the learner time to focus on the practical exercises. Visit www.digidiscover.com/downloads and click on the manual you are using.

Files should be saved in an ICDL Professional folder in 'Documents' on your computer.

Introduction

The International Computer Driving Licence (ICDL) Professional is a series of digital skills modules developed to improve your employment prospects, capability and build on your existing knowledge. You can add to your learner profile using any combination of successfully completed modules tailored to suit your workplace or business requirements. The subjects we will cover in this book include advanced word processing, management spreadsheets, financial spreadsheets, advanced presentation, and advanced database.

The modules, formerly known as Advanced European Computer Driving Licence (ECDL), which covered Microsoft Word, Excel, PowerPoint, and Access applications, have become part of the ICDL Professional series of computer modules. At the time of writing, there are fifteen separate modules, with a new e-commerce module soon to become available.

The word processing guidance we'll cover in this book is designed to help you develop your understanding of Microsoft Word features, possibly in preparation for your advanced word processing exam. You can add successful completion of this module and exam to your ICDL Professional learner profile. Please be aware, though, that the content of this book is only a companion to your preparation for this exam.

To get the most out of this book, I recommend that you have access to Microsoft Office 2016 or later as many of the core features and illustrations involve the latest Microsoft 365 applications using Windows on a PC computer. The new additions to Microsoft Word include sharing and collaboration features, cloud-based services such as OneDrive, the Tell Me feature, Smart Lookup for researching topics, new chart types, translator tools, and keyboard shortcuts.

The ribbon is similar to previous versions of Microsoft Word apart from a few changes made over the years, such as the Editor and Accessibility features. For the purposes of this book, the core components covered in the exams can be used with earlier versions of Microsoft Word.

When I began learning advanced word processing, I often spent long moments scanning the groups, tabs, ribbons, and different buttons displayed on the screen, searching for the right function. I was familiar with the software's layout but struggled to make use of its less obvious features. The practical aspects of the application evaded me, and I became frustrated and disheartened. Acquiring the skills and knowledge I needed to perform tasks effectively proved to be a long, laborious endeavour.

As I became familiar with its many advanced features, I found that there was a simpler way of learning. Understand what I was doing, why it was necessary, examples of how I might apply it to real-life situations, step-by-step tasks that needed to be achieved to complete the material, and revising what I had previously learned. This is why I have written this book. I hope to share my knowledge with readers that may help them improve their existing skills using Microsoft Office.

I hope that you find this book helpful. It may seem daunting at first, but learn steps one at a time. If there are parts that prove challenging, take note of it and move on, reviewing it later with a new perspective.

Microsoft Word is available for PC and Mac. Many of the practical exercises outlined in this book are described for Windows PC users. Mac users may find some of the steps, tools, dialog boxes and features have different names or are positioned elsewhere on screen. If you encounter any tools that are alternatively named on a Mac, it may require some time to search for them. The basic functionality is the same, it may be displayed on-screen elsewhere.

Microsoft Word is used to create documents for letters, flyers, email templates, newsletters, essays, reports, articles and many more applications. In business, users can collaborate and share projects, revise and review important material, perform internet research on relevant topics and use translation services.

Independent sole traders, entrepreneurs, administrative staff, managers, and retailers are just some of the business users of Microsoft Word. Advanced word processing skills allow readers to build on their existing understanding of the application, enhance their career prospects, and make performing repetitive tasks easier and more efficient.

Students can also benefit from learning advanced word processing techniques. Whether they want to improve their knowledge of researching and citations, indexing and tables of figures for essays, or learn how to reference material from books, articles, and websites, acquiring the necessary skills required to do this is provided in this book.

How to use this book

I have divided the book into seven parts, each one containing a number of easily navigable sections:

Advanced Word Processing will cover:

Section 1 – Formatting. Here, you will learn how to apply advanced formatting features to text, paragraphs, and entire documents using a range of different editing tools. Find out how to position elements such as images relative to text, use advanced find and replace functions to search and edit documents, and adjust column widths, spacing, and layouts.

Section 2 – Tables. This section explains how to apply different designs to tables; adjust cell margins, sizes, and positioning; and convert text to tables and tables back into text. You will also learn how to sort a table by columns and apply advanced formatting features.

Section 3 – Referencing. In this section, you will learn about referencing features including captions, footnotes, endnotes, and citations. Find out how to create a bibliography, table of contents, table of figures, as well as indexes and bookmarks in documents. Discover how to use fields to create forms and apply a range of settings to restrict editing, protect documents, and save files as templates.

Section 4 – Mail Merge. This section provides guidance on how to prepare customised letters for different recipients. Learn how to create and edit a data source; use ask fields to prompt mail-merge users to enter information; create if…then…else fields to decide what letters specific recipients will receive; and merge letters for delivery.

Section 5 – Linking. In Section 5, you will find out how to link external files such as spreadsheets and charts to documents; place unlinked external files into documents with embedding; and remove links to external files.

Section 6 – Automation. Here, you'll learn how to use automated features and apply them to documents to save time and work more efficiently. You will gain the skills you require to apply consistent formatting to documents using AutoFormat; discover shortcuts when editing text using

AutoCorrect and AutoText; create buttons that carry out recorded sequences of tasks using macros; and employ macros to make repetitive tasks easier to perform.

Section 7 – Editing. In this, the final section of Advanced Word Processing, you will develop document editing skills using the tracking changes feature; learn how to compare and combine different versions of the same document and apply password protection to sensitive information; find out how to apply page layout settings, including section breaks, headers and footers, margins, and watermarks, to documents; and understand how to review documents using the spell-checker and thesaurus.

Contents

Section 1

Formatting

In this section, you will learn how to:

- Apply advanced formatting to text, paragraphs, and documents
- Position images, tables, and charts alongside paragraphs
- Search documents with advanced Find and Replace

Text Wrapping Options

Text wrapping is a feature that allows you to position objects relative to text in a document. Objects can be placed so that the text can be on the right, left or both sides of the object. Text wrapping is practical when you want to position images neatly alongside text. This can improve the appearance of a document making it easier to understand.

1. Open the **Keep Active** document

2. Right-click on the picture and select **Wrap Text**

3. Select **More Layout Options**

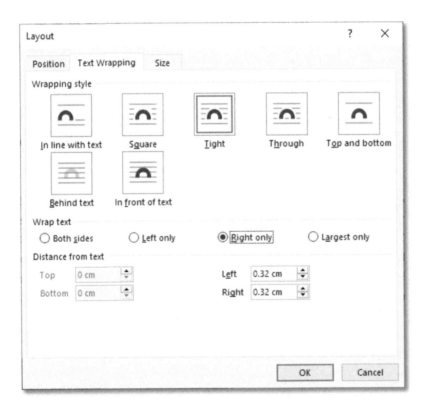

4. Select a **Wrapping Style** of **Tight**

5. Choose to **Wrap Text** to the **Right Only**

6. Click **OK**

7. Click and drag the photograph until it is positioned to the left of the text

8. Right-click on the picture again and choose **Wrap Text**

9. Select **More Layout Options**

10. Choose a **Wrapping Style** of **Behind Text**

11. The image is now behind the text

12. Click **OK**

13. Save the document as **Text Wrapping** and close it

Positioning Objects

Objects can be positioned so the text appears above and below the object. For example, when you want to include an image to accompany an article, the image can be positioned beneath a paragraph and above the following paragraph. Diagrams and drawn objects can be positioned the same way as charts.

1. Open the document **Walking**

2. Create a **Chart** in the **Illustrations** group on the **Insert** tab

3. Choose **Clustered Column Chart**

4. Click **OK**

5. Accept the default values for the chart spreadsheet

6. On the **Format** tab, click on **Position**

7. Choose **Position in Middle Centre with Square Text Wrapping**

8. Click and drag the chart below the paragraph of the text beginning "Although dieting is popular..."

9. Select the **Chart Title** and enter "Exercise."

10. On the **Chart Design** tab in the **Data** group, select **Edit Data**

11. Change the **Series 1** value to **Jan**, **Series 2** value to **Feb**, and the **Series 3** value to **Mar**

12. Change the **Category 1** value to **Dieting, Category 2** value to **Aerobic Training, Category 3** to **Flexibility** and **Category 4** to **Body Toning**

13. Keep the numerical values the same

14. Position the cursor before the third paragraph titled **Aerobic Training**

15. On the **Insert** tab in the **Illustrations** group, click on **SmartArt**

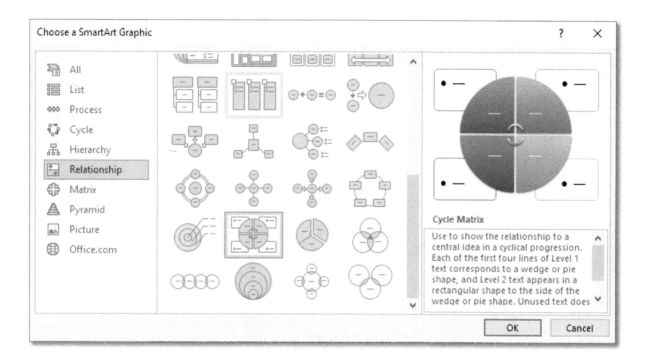

16. Select **Relationship** and choose **Cycle Matrix**

17. Click **OK**

18. Type **Dieting, Aerobic Training, Flexibility** and **Body Toning** into each segment with a brief entry describing each topic

19. Right-click on the **SmartArt Graphic** and select **Wrap Text,** and choose **More Layout Options**

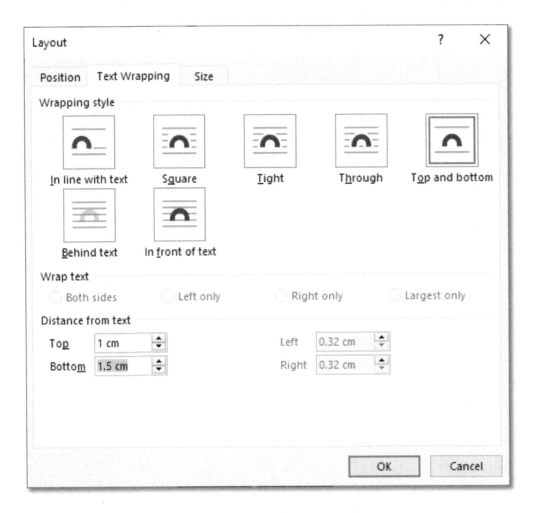

20. On the **Text Wrapping** tab, select **Top and Bottom**

21. Under **Distance from Text,** enter **1cm** for **Top** and **1.5cm** for **Bottom**

22. Click **OK**

23. Resize the **SmartArt Graphic** so that it is positioned in the middle of the **Aerobic Training** paragraph

24. Place the cursor after the **Mental Well Being** title

25. On the **Insert** tab in the **Illustrations** group, select **Shapes**

26. Under **Callouts,** select **Thought Bubble: Cloud**

27. Click and drag to create the shape while holding down the **Alt** key

28. On the **Shape Format** tab in the **Arrange** group, select **Wrap Text** and choose **Behind Text**

29. On the **Shape Format** tab in the **Shape Styles** group, select **Shape Fill** and choose **More Fill Colours**

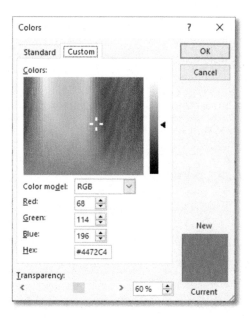

30. Adjust the **Transparency** to **60%** using the slider and click **OK**

31. This has positioned the shape behind the text

32. Save the document as **Chart** and leave it open

Positioning Tables

Tables can be aligned to the left, right or centre of the text. Text wrapping can also be applied to tables. This helpful feature allows you to align tables alongside text in a document. For example, by changing a setting in table properties, a table can be aligned to the left of a body of text.

1. Open the document **Chart**

2. On the **Insert** tab, create a table with three rows and five columns and position it below the **Aerobic Training** paragraph

3. On the **Layout** tab, click on **Properties**

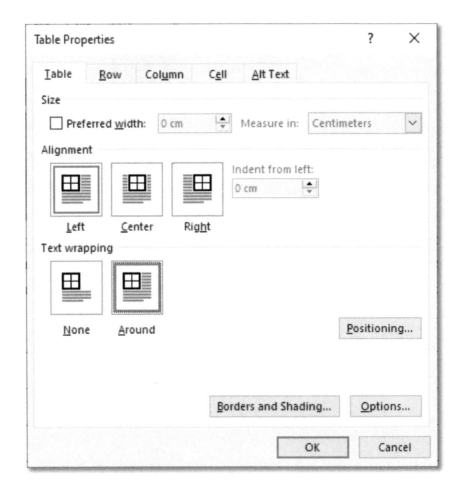

4. Select **Text Wrapping** of **Around**

5. Click **OK**

6. Click and drag the table over the **Aerobic Training** paragraph of text

7. Click and drag the corner edge of the table to resize it in line with the paragraph text

8. The text will align to the right and beneath the table

9. Enter the following details for the table:

Mon	Tue	Wed	Thu	Fri
1 mile	2 miles	1.5 miles	Rest Day	3 miles
2 miles	3 miles	1 mile	Rest Day	2.5 miles

10. Save the document as **Table** and close it

Find and Replace

Advanced find and replace features enable you to search a document according to specified criteria. This includes finding and replacing whole words, text formatted with uppercase text, types of font and paragraph styles. The find and replace function can also find paragraph formatting, such as paragraph marks (when the Enter key is pressed for a new paragraph) and indenting (when the tab key is pressed).

1. Open the **Walking** document

2. On the **Home** tab in the **Editing** group, click on **Replace**

3. Click on **More**

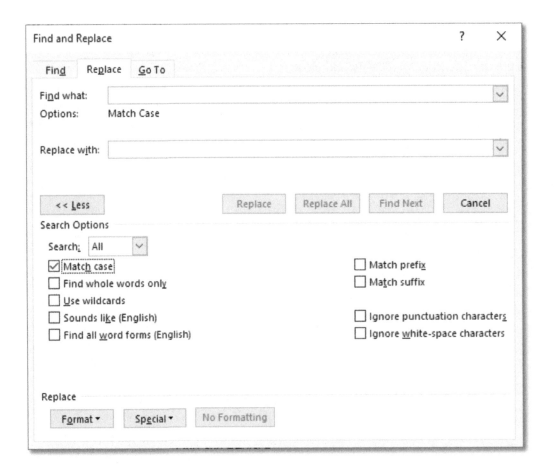

4. Click on the **Match Case** checkbox

5. In the **Find What** text box, type in "versatile."

6. In the **Replace With** text box, type in "enjoyable."

7. Click on **Replace All**

8. The search will only find a match that has the same lowercase lettering

9. Save the document and leave it open

Finding Whole Words

Whole words in a document can be found and replaced with other whole words. This is useful if you want to find an exact match of a word in a document and replace it with another. For example, you can search a document for the word "Chapter" and replace every occurrence of that word with "Section".

1. Open the **Walking** document

2. Display the **Find and Replace** dialog box

3. In the **Find What** text box, type in "readily."

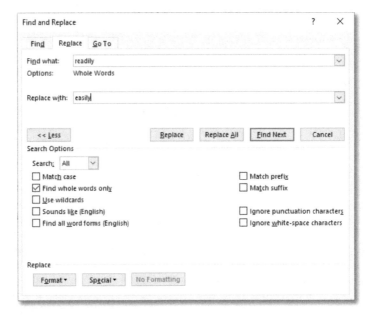

4. In the **Replace With** text box, type in "easily."

5. Select the **Find Whole Words Only** checkbox

6. Click on **Replace All**

7. Save the document and leave it open

Replacing Types of Font

Documents can be searched for specific font types and replaced with a different kind of font. This is an efficient way of changing fonts within a document and can save time when performing repetitive tasks. For instance, you may want to replace all the Times New Roman formatted text with an Arial formatted text without changing anything else. This can be achieved using the replacing types of font feature.

1. Open the **Walking** document

2. In the **Advanced Find and Replace** dialog box, under **Find,** click on **Format,** then **Font**

3. On the **Font** tab, choose **Times New Roman**

4. Click **OK**

5. In the **Find What** text box, type in "walking."

6. In the **Replace With** text box, type in "strolling."

7. Click on **Replace All**

8. Only text that is in the **Times New Roman** font will be replaced

9. Click on the **No Formatting** button to remove the format

10. Save the document

Finding Paragraph Marks

When you press the Enter key, paragraph marks appear if the Show/Hide feature is active. Paragraph marks can be replaced with alternative marks such as indents or page breaks. For instance, you may want to replace each paragraph mark with a page break so that paragraphs appear on separate pages rather than together on the same page.

1. Open the **Walking** document

2. In the **Find and Replace** dialog box, under **Find**, click on the **Special** button, then **Paragraph Mark**

3. Click on **Find Next**

4. Word will search for any paragraph marks in the text

5. Click inside the **Replace with** text box

6. Select the **Special** button, then choose **Manual Page Break**

7. Click on **Replace All**

8. This will replace paragraph marks with page breaks throughout the document

9. Save the document and close it

Paste Special

Paste special can copy and paste text according to specific criteria, e.g. keeping the same formatting when pasting. The same formatting of the original copied text can be maintained, or the formatting of the original text can be merged with the destination text.

1. Open the **Work Life Balance** document

2. Highlight the heading and copy it

3. Highlight the first paragraph beginning, "Stress is known to be one…."

4. On the **Home** tab, click on the **Paste** drop-down arrow

5. Under **Paste Options**, select **Merge Formatting**

6. The formatting of the copied text is merged with the first paragraph formatting

7. Save the document

Paste Unformatted Text

1. Highlight the heading again

2. Copy the text and select **Paste Special**

3. Place the cursor below the heading

4. On the **Home** tab, click on the **Paste** drop-down arrow

5. Under **Paste Options**, select **Paste Special**

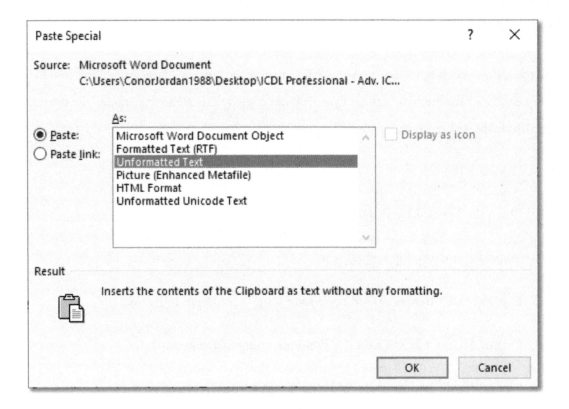

6. Choose **Unformatted Text**

7. Click **OK**

8. This pastes the text without formatting

9. Save the document

Line Spacing

Line spacing can be set to specify minimum spacing options, e.g. lines being at least 6pt apart. Spacing before and after lines of text can be adjusted.

1. With the **Work Life Balance** document still open, highlight the first paragraph

2. Click on the **Paragraph Dialog Box Launcher**

3. In the **Spacing** group in the **Line Spacing** drop-down box, choose **At Least**

4. Choose **At: 12pt**

5. Click **OK**

6. This will ensure there is 12pt spacing between lines

7. Open the **Paragraph Dialog Box** again by clicking on the arrow to the right of the **Paragraph** group

8. In the **Line Spacing** drop-down box, choose **Exactly**

9. Click **OK**

10. This makes text appear evenly spaced

11. Open the **Paragraph Dialog Box** again, and in the **Line Spacing** drop-down box, choose **Multiple** and for **At** choose **2**

12. This applies spacing as a multiple of the current font size. The larger the text, the greater the spacing between lines.

13. Save the document and close it

Pagination

The **Widow/Orphan** checkbox stops Word from displaying the last part of a paragraph on a new page (**Widow**) or leaving the start of a paragraph at the bottom of the previous page (**Orphan**). This feature can ensure that text in a document appears together on a page. Without this feature, the start of a paragraph will appear on one page and the rest on the next.

1. Open the **Getting Fit for the New Year** document

2. Open the **Paragraph** dialog box

3. Click on the **Line and Page Breaks** tab

4. Uncheck the **Widow/Orphan** control check box

5. Click **OK**

6. Notice the effects this has on the document

7. Open the **Paragraph** dialog box

8. Click on the **Line and Page Breaks** tab

9. Click on the **Widow/Orphan** control check box

10. Click **OK**

11. The control is now on; notice the effect it has on the document

12. Highlight the paragraph titled **Running**

13. Open the **Paragraph** dialog box

14. Select the **Keep Lines Together** checkbox

15. Click **OK**

16. This has kept the paragraph text together on the second page with the heading on the first page

17. Open the **Paragraph** dialog box again

18. Deselect the **Keep Lines Together** checkbox

19. Select the **Page Break Before** checkbox and click **OK**

20. A page break has been placed after the **Running** paragraph heading

21. With the paragraph still selected, uncheck the **Page Break Before** checkbox

22. Select the **Keep with Next** checkbox and click **OK**

23. This keeps the paragraph title with the paragraph text

24. Save the document and close it

Outline Numbering

Numbering for lists can be adjusted with outline numbering. If you have a numbered list and want to use an indent, you can apply a different type of numbering to the indented line of text. This is used when different formatting in a list is needed. For example, you can apply i) ii) iii) style formatting to the first level of a list, and 1) 2) 3) to the second level of a list and so on.

1. Open a new document

2. On the **Home** tab, click on **Multilevel List**

3. Choose **Define New Multilevel List**

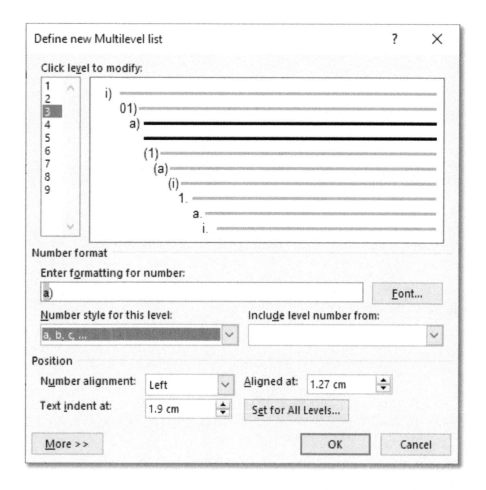

4. On the **Number Style For This Level** drop-down box, choose the **i), ii), iii)** format

5. Select level **2**

6. Choose the **01, 02, 03** format

7. Select level **3**

8. Choose the **a), b), c)** format

9. Click on the **Font** button

10. Choose a dark grey text colour

11. Click **OK**

12. Click **OK** again

13. Use the **Tab** key to move to the **Second** and **Third List Level**

14. Create the following list:

    i) Business Management

        01 Finance

            a) Accounts

15. Save and close the document

Styles

Styles can apply a consistent format to text in a document. Font for titles, headings, and body text can have the same formatting applied using styles. For example, when writing an essay, a style can be applied so that headings have a larger font size. Styles can be applied to ensure subtitles have a different colour with italics and paragraphs containing smaller text suitable for reading.

1. Open the **How to get stuck while writing** document

2. Highlight the main heading

3. Click on the **Styles Dialog Box Launcher** located to the right of the **Styles** group on the **Home** tab

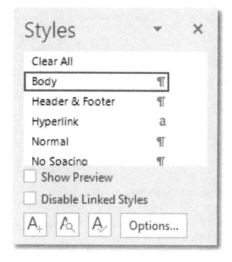

4. Click on the **New Style** button on the bottom left corner of the **Styles** panel

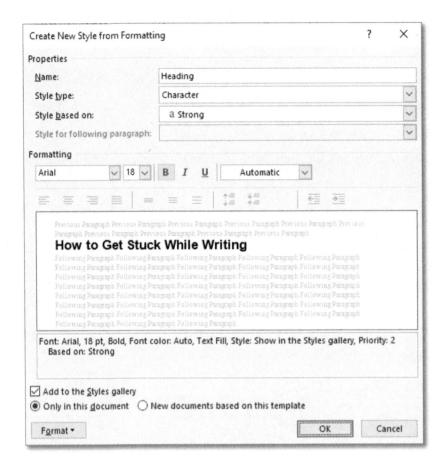

5. In the **Name** property type **Heading**

6. For **Style Type,** choose **Character**

7. For **Style Based On** select **Strong**

8. Format the text as **Arial, 18pt, Bold**

9. Click **OK**

10. Use the **Ctrl** key to highlight each of the headings

11. On the **Home** tab in the **Styles** group, choose **Heading** from the styles available

12. This will apply the **Heading** style to all the paragraph headings

13. Display the **Styles** panel again

14. Click on the **Arrow** to the right of the **Heading** character style that has been applied to each heading

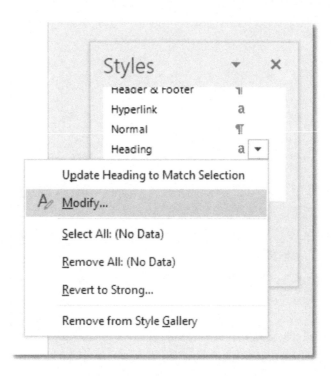

15. Select **Modify** from the list of options that appear

16. Click on **Format** and choose **Font**

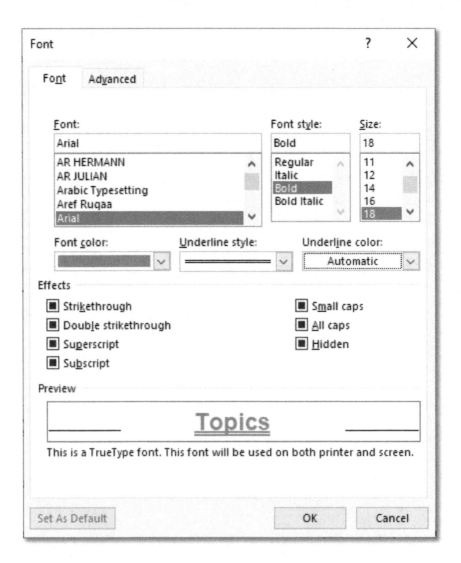

17. Change the **Font Color** to a **Dark Grey**

18. Apply a **Double Line Underline Style** with an **Underline Color** of **Automatic**

19. Click **OK**

20. The character style has been modified

21. Display the **Styles** panel again

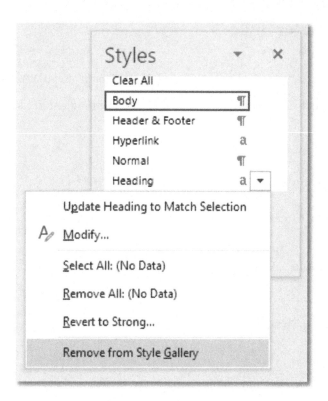

22. Click on the **Arrow** beside the **Heading** style

23. Choose **Remove from Style Gallery**

24. The style has been deleted

25. Save the document and leave it open

39

Creating a Character Style

Character styles are an efficient way of formatting a document. Character styles are types of font that can be applied to text in a document. This setting can be adjusted using the styles formatting dialog box.

1. Ensure the **How to get stuck while writing** document is open

2. Create a **New Style**

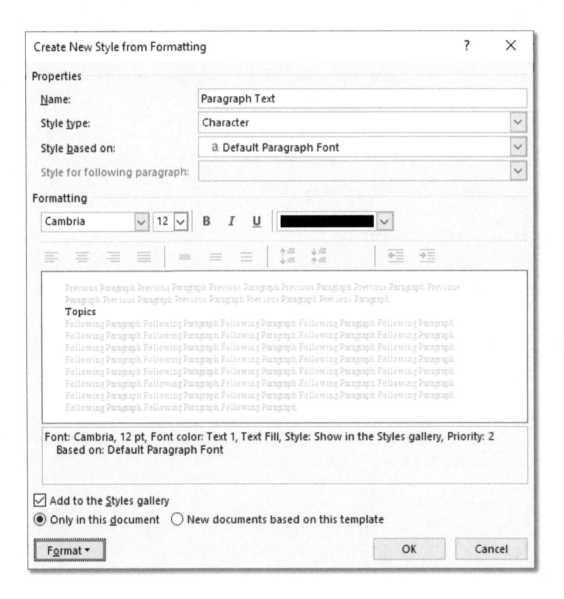

3. Name it **Paragraph Text**

4. Choose **Character** for **Style Type**

5. For **Style Based On,** choose **Default Paragraph Font**

6. Change the format to **Cambria, 12pt** and colour of **Black**

7. Click **OK**

8. Apply it to each paragraph

9. Save the document and leave it open

Updating Styles

A character font can be applied to other text sections in a document by matching styles. This is an efficient way of applying a similar style to parts of the document containing similar content, such as paragraphs.

1. Ensure the **How to get stuck while writing** document is open

2. Highlight the second paragraph beginning "Distractions become common..."

3. Click on the arrow beside the **Paragraph Text**

4. Choose **Update Paragraph Text to Match Selection**

5. The **Paragraph Text** style has been updated to match the style of the selected paragraph

6. Leave the document open

Modifying Styles

Existing styles can be adjusted, including font and paragraph settings. This feature is useful when you want to change the style and maintain a similar layout in a document.

1. With the document still open, after the **Normal** style, click on the drop-down arrow and choose **Modify**

2. Format the **Paragraph Text** style to **Times New Roman, 12pt, Justified**

3. Click on **Format** and choose **Border**

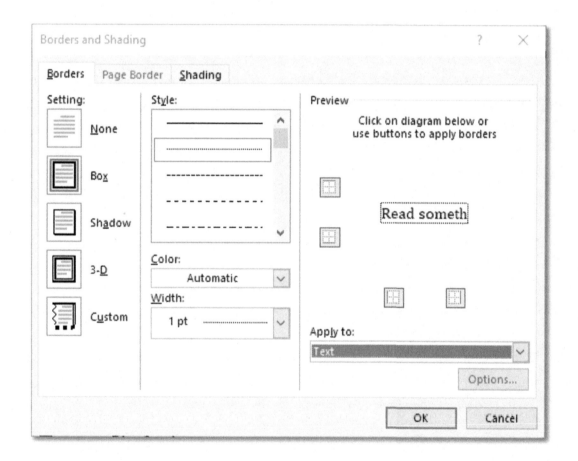

4. Under **Setting,** choose **Box**

5. For **Style,** choose the second dotted line **Style**

6. Change the **Width** to **1pt**

7. Click **OK**

8. Highlight the first paragraph in the document and apply this style to the text

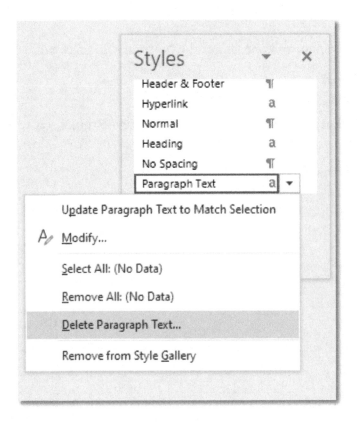

9. Click on the **Arrow** beside the **Paragraph Text** style

10. Select **Delete Paragraph Text**

11. The style has been deleted

12. Save the document as **Styles** and close it

Alternative Text

Alternative text describes an image, diagram, object, or chart in a document to people with eyesight difficulties. This accessibility feature uses a screen reader to describe the object using text to speech software allowing the user to understand what is on screen. This feature can be used when presenting information to visually impaired people.

1. With the **Styles** document open, select the **Pen** image positioned above the **Writing Methods** paragraph

2. On the **Review** tab in the **Accessibility** group, select **Check Accessibility**

3. Choose **Alt Text** to display the alternative text pane on the right of the screen

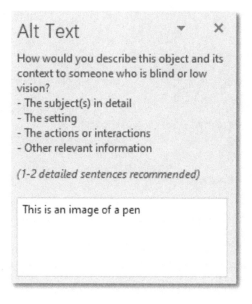

4. In the textbox provided, type in "This is an image of a pen."

5. To allow the **Screen Reader** to read the message aloud, turn on **Narrator** using the built-in **Windows Narrator**

6. When **Narrator** is activated, hover the mouse pointer over the image, and the **Alternative Text** will be read aloud

7. Save the document

Multiple Column Layouts

Paragraphs can be reformatted to display as multiple column layouts. The number of columns on a page, the spacing between them and their widths can be changed. For example, this feature is useful when writing articles or preparing documents for a newsletter or internet blog.

1. Open the document **Introducing Flexibility into your Routine**

2. On the **Home** tab, click on the **Show/Hide** button

3. Highlight all the text using the **Ctrl+A** keyboard shortcut

4. On the **Layout** tab in the **Page Setup** group, click on **Columns** and choose **2**

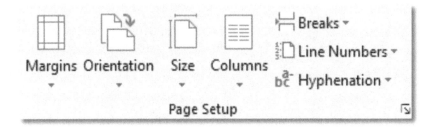

5. Change the number of columns by clicking on the **Columns** button and choose **3**

6. Return the layout to **2** columns

7. Place the cursor at the start of the second paragraph

8. On the **Layout** tab, click on **Breaks**

9. Choose **Column Break**

10. This will put the second paragraph at the top of the second column

11. Delete the **Column Break** by highlighting the **Column Break** and pressing the **Delete** key

12. Insert a **Continuous Break** after the first paragraph to display the text in each column evenly

13. Delete the continuous column break

14. Save the document as **Columns** and close it

Column Widths & Spacing

The width and spacing of each column can be set to change the appearance of text on a page. This can make the text in each column easier to read and make the overall appearance presentable.

1. With the **Columns** document still open, place the cursor at the beginning of the first column, beginning "Flexibility is an essential component..."

2. On the **Layout** tab in the **Page Setup** group, click on **Columns**

3. Choose **More Columns**

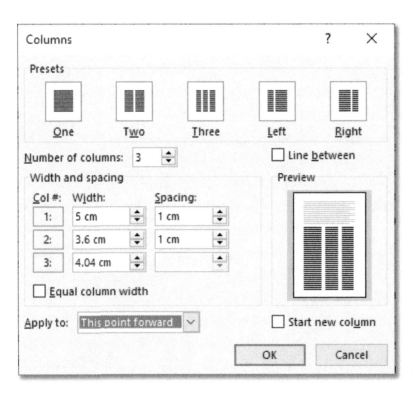

4. Select **3** for the **Number of Columns**

5. Deselect the **Equal Column Width** checkbox

6. Enter in the above **Width** and **Spacing** values in **cm**

7. Click **OK**

8. Notice the effect this has on each column

9. Highlight each column

10. On the **Layout** tab, click on **Columns**

11. Choose **More Columns**

12. Click on the **Line Between** checkbox

13. Click on the **Equal Column Width** checkbox

14. Notice the line between each column and equal widths in the document

15. Place the cursor before the second paragraph beginning with "Regular…."

16. On the **Layout** tab, click on **Breaks**

17. Choose **Column Break**

18. Notice the layout of the column at the top of the third page

19. On the **Home** tab, select the **Show/Hide** button

20. Highlight the **Column Break**

21. Use the **Backspace** key to delete it

22. Save the document as **Columns**

Revision - Section 1

1. Open the document **Presents**

2. Apply a wrapping style of **Tight**

3. Position the object to the **Right** of the first paragraph

4. Save the document as **Text Wrapping**

5. Open the document **Media**

6. Apply text wrapping of **Top and Bottom** and position it below the first paragraph

7. Find the **Arial** font and replace it with **Times New Roman**

8. Find **Paragraph Marks** in the text

9. Copy the title "Media."

10. Use **Paste Special** to **Merge Formatting** with the first paragraph

11. Apply **Line Spacing** of **At Least** 6pt to the document

12. Apply the **Widow/Orphan** control to the document

13. Define a **New Multilevel List** and apply different numbering for each level

14. Apply this numbering to the list underneath "Benefits of Media."

15. Apply a style of **Arial 16pt Bold** to each heading in the document and name it **Heading**

16. Create a **Character** style of **Arial 12pt** to the body text and name it **Character**

17. Divide the text into **Three** columns with **1cm** spacing

18. Resize the image, so it is placed in the top right-hand corner

19. Save the document and close it

Summary

Formatting

In this section, you have learned how to:

- Apply consistent styles to headings, paragraphs and font in documents
- Use text wrapping to reposition images and tables in relation to text
- Search and replace text based on settings such as font, case, whole words and paragraph marks

Section 2

Tables

In this section, you will learn how to:

- Adjust table design and appearance

- Format table properties and contents

- Position tables relative to text and paragraphs

Table Styles

A range of styles can be applied to tables using pre-set formats. Finding a table style that will suit your document can be achieved quickly with the range of built-in styles available.

1. Open a **New Document**

2. On the **Insert** tab in the **Tables** group, create a table with three rows and four columns

3. On the **Table Design** tab, click on the drop-down arrow

4. Choose **Grid Table 4 – Accent 2**

Jan	Feb	Mar	Apr
25,500	23,550	25,500	22,000
21,550	18,500	19,500	15,400

5. Fill in the above information into the table

6. Change the table style to **Grid Table 4 – Accent 5**

7. Save the document as **Table** and leave it open

Merge & Split Cells/Table

Cells can be divided into two or more cells using the split function. This feature may be used when creating a table that requires separate cells for data entry. The merge feature joins two or more cells together. This feature may be used when creating a table header. A table can also be split into two tables. This is useful when a separate table containing different information is needed.

1. With the document still open, highlight the first **Jan** and **Feb** cells in the first row

2. On the **Layout** tab, click on **Merge Cells**

3. The cells have been merged into one cell

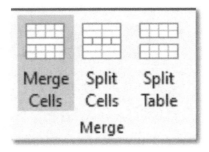

4. With the cell still selected, click on **Split Cells**

5. Choose **Number of Columns 2**

6. Click **OK**

7. The cells have been split into two

8. With the cursor in the second row, click on **Split Table**

9. This splits the table into two

10. **Undo** the **Split**

11. Save the document as **Table**

Cell Margins

The margins of cells in a table can be adjusted using table options. The top, bottom, left, and right margins are measured in centimetres. Spacing can be applied to cells in a table to change its appearance. Cells in a table can also be resized according to the requirements of the table.

1. Open the **Quarterly Sales** document

2. Click on the table

3. On the **Layout** tab, select **Properties**

4. In the **Table Properties** dialog box, choose **Cell** tab

5. Under **Vertical Alignment,** choose **Top**. This will place the text at the top of each selected cell

6. Click on **Options**

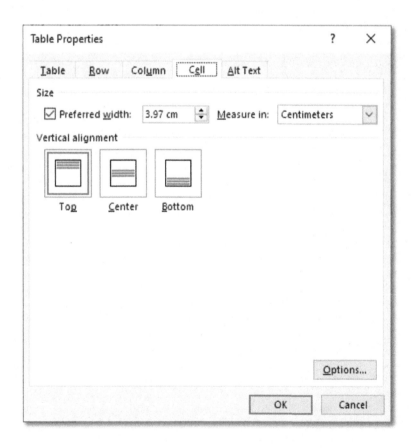

7. Choose **Same As Whole Table**

8. Click **OK** and click **OK** again

9. On the **Layout** tab in the **Alignment** group, select **Cell Margins**

10. Change the **Default Cell Margins** to the following settings:

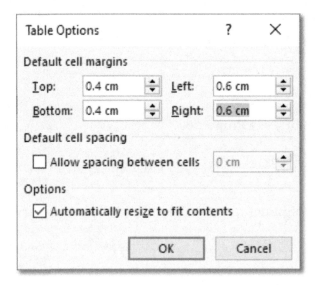

11. Click **OK**

12. Save the document as **Table2** and close it

Aligning Text

Text can be aligned top, middle, and bottom as well as left, centre and right in a cell. This changes the appearance of text in a table and is often used for headers. For example, the text direction can be altered so headings appear vertically aligned with text reading upwards rather than horizontal alignment.

1. With the **Table2** document open, highlight the table in the document

2. On the **Layout** tab in the **Alignment** group, select **Align Top Left**

3. Notice how it aligns the text contained within the table

4. Highlight the month headers in the table

5. Click on the **Text Direction** button to change the text direction to **Vertical**

6. Notice how the headers text direction has changed to vertical

7. Highlight the numerical values

8. On the **Layout** tab in the **Alignment** group, select **Align Center**

9. Save the document as **Aligned** and close it

Repeat Header Row

Headers in tables can be repeated if the table continues onto a new page. This means that the headers for tables will appear at the top of each new page if your table exceeds the limits of one page.

1. Open the **Quarterly Sales** document

2. Highlight the entire table

3. On the **Layout** tab in the **Rows & Columns** group, click on **Insert Below**

4. Insert the rows until new rows are created on the second page

5. On the **Layout** tab in the **Table** group, click on **Properties**

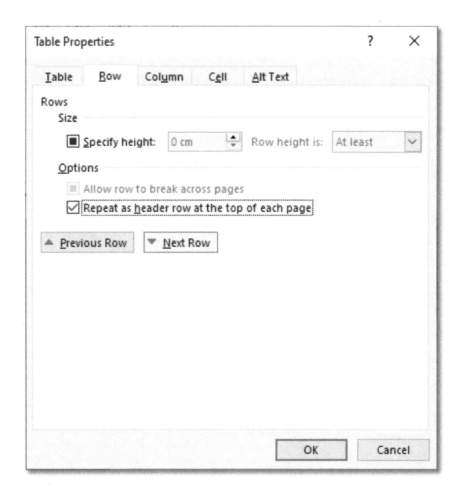

6. Click on the **Row** tab

7. Under **Options,** select the **Repeat As Header Row at the Top of Each Page** checkbox

8. This feature repeats the row headers at the top of each page

9. Highlight the last row on the first page

10. Uncheck **Allow Row to Break Across Pages**

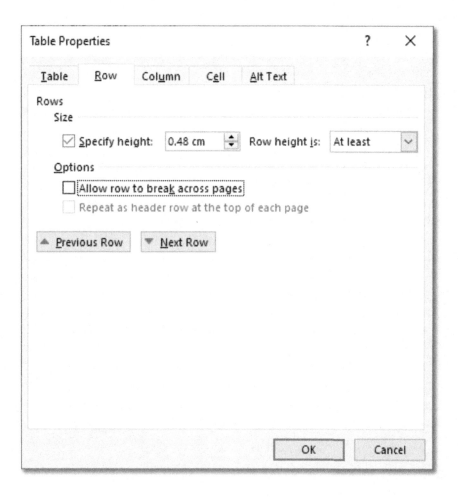

11. This keeps the data in the rows together

12. Select this check box again to turn that control on

13. Click **OK**

14. Save the document as **Repeated Header** and close it

Sorting a Table

You can sort tables in ascending or descending alphabetical order. If your table has a list of names, the surnames can be sorted in ascending order. For example, a table containing contact details for a company can be sorted with surnames that are towards the beginning of the alphabet appearing first and those towards the end appearing further down the table.

1. Open the document **Contact Details**

2. Highlight the table

3. On the **Layout** tab in the **Data** group, select **Sort**

4. Sort the table by **Surname Descending**

5. With this setting, the table will only be sorted by **Surname**

6. Under **Then By** enter **First Name Ascending**

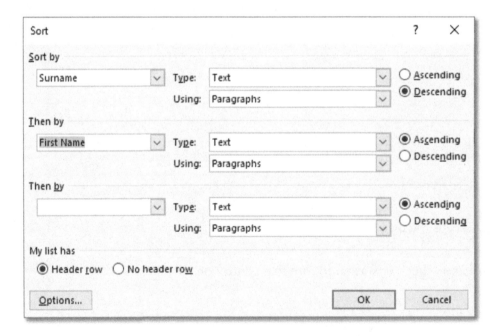

7. Click **OK**

8. Click **OK** and save the document as **Sort**

60   © Conor Jordan 2022

Converting Text to a Table

Text divided by commas, tabs, paragraphs, or other separators can be converted into a table. This is a more efficient way of converting text in a document into a table without manually entering the information into a new table. For example, suppose you have a list of contact details saved in a document separated by commas. In that case, this information can be converted into a table.

1. Open a new **Word document**

2. Type in the following text:

First Name, Surname, Address, Telephone

Mary, Walsh, Glen Road, 49283749

Tom, Mathews, Glenview, 48573948

Frank, Jones, Main Street, 48573674

Sean, Dunne, Park West, 48573648

3. Highlight all the text

4. On the **Insert** tab, click on **Table** and choose **Convert Text to Table**

5. Choose **Tabs** for **Separate Text At**

6. Click **OK**

7. Save the document as **Converted**

8. Create another document with the following information separated by tabs:

First name	George	Henry	Sarah	Lisa
Surname	Smith	Dunne	Walsh	Jones
Telephone	(04) 3746574	(03) 3746574	(06) 5746374	(06) 3847575

9. Highlight all the text

10. On the **Insert** tab, click on **Table** and choose **Convert Text to Table**

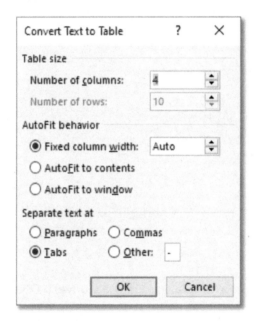

11. Under **Table Size,** choose **Number of Columns** as **4**

12. Choose **Tabs** for **Separate Text At**

13. Click **OK**

14. Another table has been created

15. Save the document and leave it open

Converting a Table to Text

A table containing information in a document can be converted into text separated by paragraph marks, tabs, commas, or another separator. This is useful when extracting the information from a table and displaying it as text.

1. Open the **Converted** document

2. Select the first table separated by **Commas**

3. On the **Layout** tab in the **Data** group, click on **Table**

4. Click on **Convert to Text**

5. Choose **Commas**

6. Click **OK**

7. The first table is converted to text separated by commas

8. Select the second table

9. On the **Layout** tab in the **Data** group, click on **Convert to Text**

10. Choose **Tabs**

11. Click **OK**

12. Save the document and close it

Revision - Section 2

1. Open the document **Sales**

2. **Split the Table** by separating the headers from the data

3. **Merge** the Saturday and Sunday columns and label the heading **Weekend**

4. Apply **Cell Margins** of 0.3cm

5. Change the **Text Direction** of the headers

6. Apply an **Align Right Centre** alignment to the headers

7. Apply the **Repeat as header row** setting to the document

8. **Sort** the values in the table in **Ascending** order

9. Save the document as **Sales Table** and close it

10. Open the document **Table**

11. Convert the **Text into a Table**

12. Convert the **Table** back into **Text**

13. Save the document and close it

Summary

Tables

In this section, you have learned how to:

- Apply different built-in designs to tables

- Resize, split and merge cells and tables

- Convert text to tables and convert tables to text

Section 3

Referencing

In this section, you will learn how to:

- Reference other works including articles, books, and websites
- Create forms for other users
- Apply security features to documents

Captions

A caption is text that describes an image. Text can be set to appear above or below an image. This is a helpful way of labelling images in a document. The position, formatting, and caption type can be changed in a document.

1. Open the document **Healthy Eating Tips**

2. Select the water image on the first page

3. On the **References** tab in the **Captions** group, click on **Insert Caption**

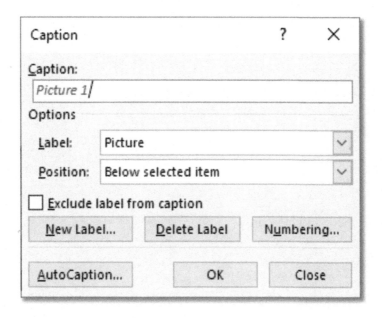

4. Click on the **New Label** button

5. Type in **Image** and click **OK**

6. Click **OK** again

7. A caption for the image has been created

8. Save the document as **Caption**

9. Select the salad image on the second page

10. On the **References** tab, click on **Insert Caption**

11. Select the **Image** label

12. Change the **Position** of the image to **Above Selected Item**

13. Click **OK** and click **OK** again

14. Another caption has been created above the salad image

15. Save the document as **Caption** and leave it open

Deleting Captions

1. Open the **Caption** dialog box again

2. Select the **Image** caption and click on **Delete Label**

3. Click **OK**

4. The label is deleted

5. Save the document and close it

Table Captions

Captions can be included to describe the contents of a table. The format, position and type of caption can be adjusted. Table captions are similar to image captions and can be formatted and positioned accordingly.

1. Open the **Sales** document

2. Select the table

3. On the **References** tab, click on **Insert Caption**

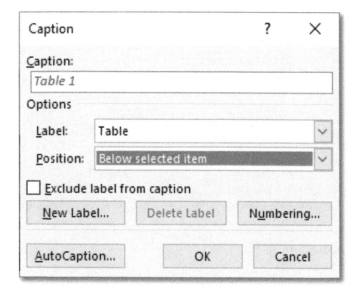

4. Change the **Position** to **Below Selected Item**

5. Click **OK**

6. Save the document as **Caption**

Caption Numbering

Different types of number formats can be applied to captions. Upper-case and lowercase Roman numerals, numbers with brackets can be applied to captions.

1. Open the **Caption** document

2. Open the **Caption** dialog box again

3. Click on **Numbering**

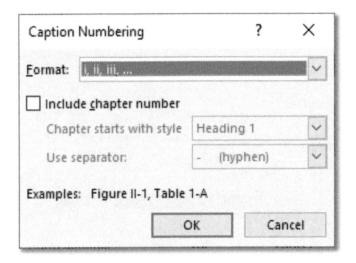

4. Change the **Format** to i, ii, iii, …

5. Click **OK**

6. Click **OK** again

7. Numbering has been applied to the caption

8. Save the document as **Table Captions**

Footnotes

Footnotes are descriptions of words or sentences in a document placed at the end of a page. A small number appears after a selected word or phrase in a body of text, and a corresponding description appears at the end of the page. The description is usually an elaboration of the word or phrase that has appeared in the body of the document.

1. Open the document **Keeping Fit in Cold Weather**

2. Place the cursor after the word "weights" in the second paragraph

3. On the **References** tab, click on **Insert Footnote**

4. Type in "Regular weights can build strength"

5. This **Footnote** is placed at the end of the page

6. Place the cursor after the word "Exercise" in the third paragraph

7. On the **References** tab, click on **Insert Footnotes**

8. Type in "Bodyweight exercises are also beneficial"

9. This **Footnote** is placed at the end of the page

10. Save the document as **Footnotes** and leave it open

Endnotes

Endnotes are similar to footnotes, but the descriptions appear at the end of the document rather than at the end of the page. For example, suppose you want to reference a sentence in a body of text. You can insert an endnote to number the sentence and place a corresponding description at the end of the document.

1. Open the **Footnote** document

2. Place the cursor after the word "iso- kinetic" in the fourth paragraph

3. On the **References** tab, click on **Insert Endnote**

4. Type "Provides resistance equal to the force exerted"

5. This **Endnote** is placed at the end of the document

6. Return to the first **Footnote** at the end of the first page

7. Highlight the text

8. Type "Many types of exercise including bodyweight exercises are beneficial"

9. The **Footnote** has been edited

10. Save the document and close it

Convert Footnotes to Endnotes

You can convert footnotes appearing at the end of a page to endnotes. Endnotes can also be converted to footnotes so that references appear at the end of the page. This feature can be used when adjusting the referencing applied to a document.

1. Open the **Footnote** document

2. Click on the **Footnotes Dialog Box Launcher**

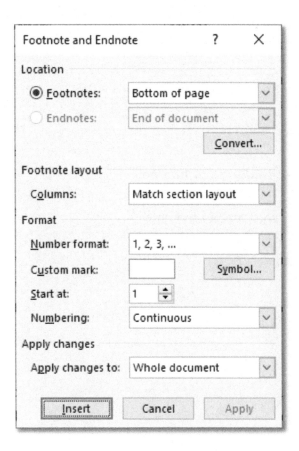

3. Click on the **Convert** button

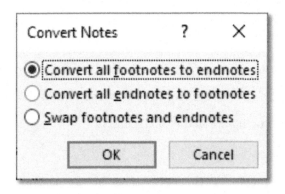

4. Select **Convert All Footnotes to Endnotes**

5. All **Footnotes** will be converted to **Endnotes**

6. Save the document as **Endnotes**

7. Open the **Footnotes and Endnotes** dialog box again

8. Click on the **Convert** button

9. Choose **Convert All Endnotes to Footnotes**

10. All endnotes will be converted to footnotes

11. Save the document and close it

Inserting Citations

A citation is a reference to a book, journal, website, article, or other published work. Once you provide Word with the information about the source of the selected text, the citation will be referenced. The citation will be placed in the correct format with the author and the year of publication included after the reference.

1. Open the document **How to get stuck while writing**

2. Highlight the text starting with "The wonderful moment…."

3. On the **References** tab, click on **Insert Citation**

4. Select **Add New Source**

5. For **Type of Source** select **Web Site**

6. For **Author**, type in Conor Jordan

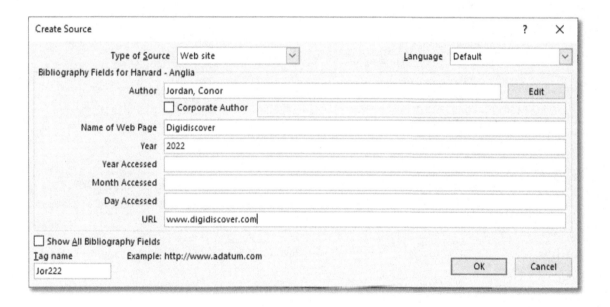

7. For **Name of Web Site** enter Digidiscover

8. For **Year** enter 2022

9. For **URL** enter www.digidiscover.com

10. Click **OK**

11. The citation is placed in the text

12. To edit a citation, right-click on the citation and select **Edit this Citation**

13. For **Add pages,** enter 2019 and **Suppress** choose **Year**

14. Click **OK**

15. Highlight the text beginning in the second paragraph

16. On the **References** tab, click on **Insert Citation** and select **Add New Source**

17. For **Type of Source,** select **Conference Proceedings**

18. Fill in the following details:

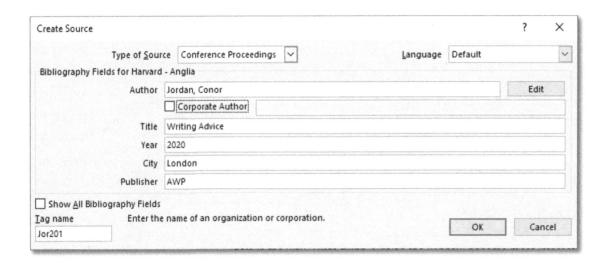

Author	Jordan, Conor
Title	Writing Advice
Pages	68
Year	2000

Conference publication name	Author Guild Manual
City	London
Publisher	AWP

19. Click **OK**

20. The citation has been added to the document

21. Save the document as **Citation** and close it

Citation Style

The citation style can be adjusted to suit the purpose of the document. There are many citation styles to choose from, including Harvard Anglia.

1. Open the **Citation** document

2. On the **References** tab in the **Citations & Bibliography** group, select **Style**

3. For **Style,** choose **Harvard - Anglia**

4. This changes the style of citation used in your document

5. On the **References** tab in the **Citations & Bibliography** group, select **Style**

6. For **Style** choose **APA**

7. The citation style has been changed again

8. Save the document

Bibliography

A bibliography is a reference placed at the end of a document containing details about the sources of material contained within a document. Bibliographies are often used for essays, reports, articles, and briefs. They contain information such as the title of the referenced material, the publisher, the date published and the page number of the source.

1. Open the **Citations** document

2. Scroll to the end of the document and insert a **Page Break**

3. Place the cursor on the last page of the document

4. On the **References** tab, select **Bibliography**

5. Choose **Bibliography**

6. This will place the **Bibliography** at the end of the document

7. Click on the arrow beside the **Website** citation in the second paragraph

8. Edit the **Web Site** source to the year 2019

9. Right-click on the **Bibliography**

10. Select **Update Field**

11. The **Bibliography** has been updated

12. Save the document as **Referenced**

Table of Contents

A table of contents provides information about what content appears on specific pages in a document. This is useful when you have created a long document with many different sections or chapters and reference them at the beginning of the document. Before creating a table of contents, ensure that a consistent style is applied to each heading and title to make the table of contents.

1. Open the document **Festival Survival Guide**

2. Format the paragraph headings using the **Heading 1** style

3. Insert a page break before the heading using the shortcut **Ctrl+Enter**

4. On the **References** tab, click on **Table of Contents**

5. Select **Custom Table of Contents**

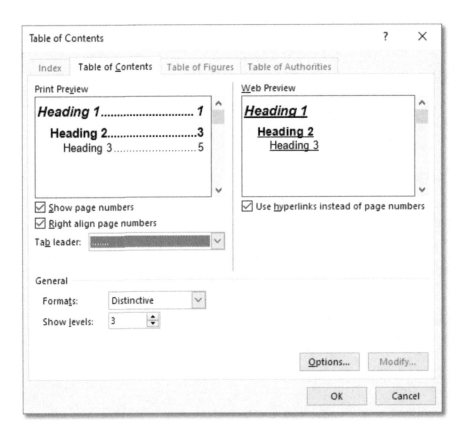

6. For **Format** select **Distinctive**

7. Change the **Tab Leader** to ......

8. Insert page breaks before each heading

9. Right-click on the **Table of Contents**

10. Click on **Update Field**

11. Select **Update Entire Table**

12. Click **OK**

13. The table of contents has been updated

14. Enter a header of **Table of Contents**

15. Highlight the table of contents

16. Locate the **References** tab in the **Table of Contents** group

17. Select **Table of Contents**

18. Select **Custom Table of Contents**

19. Click on **Options**

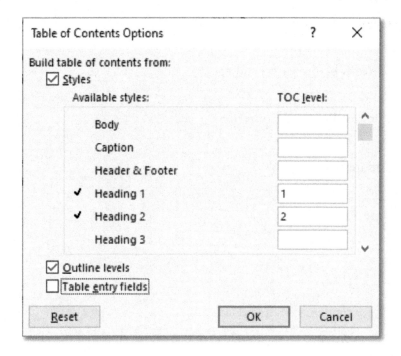

20. Delete the **TOC Level** for **Heading 3**

21. **Heading 3** will no longer be used for the table of contents

22. Click **OK** and click **OK** again

23. Select **OK** to change the table of contents

24. Save the document as **Table of Contents**

Table of Figures

A table of figures lists the images, charts or objects contained within a document. This is placed after the table of contents and describes what pages the objects in the document appear. The table of figures can be formatted to suit the document's style. For example, when a report contains charts explaining the accompanying text, each caption applied to the charts will appear as a list after the table of contents.

1. Open the **Table of Contents** document

2. Insert a **Caption** of **Figure** for each of the images

3. Place the cursor just after the table of contents

4. Locate the **References** tab in the **Captions** group

5. Click on **Insert Table of Figures**

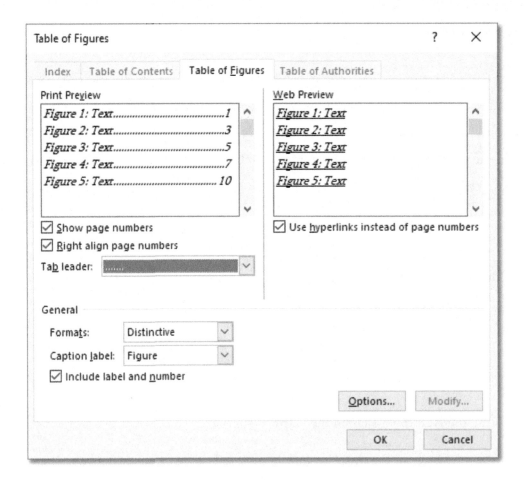

6. Change the **Tab Leader** to dots

7. Change the **Formats** to **Distinctive**

8. Deselect the checkbox **Use Hyperlinks Instead of Page Numbers**

9. Click on the **Options** button

10. Click **OK**

11. A table of figures will be inserted into the document

12. Include a heading of **Table of Figures** above the table

13. Save the document as **Table of Figures**

Indexes

An index can be inserted at the end of a document to show the pages where certain words or phrases appear in the text. This is often used in books. When readers want to find out where a specific topic is covered in a document, they can check the index for information. Indexed words can be cross-referenced to show what page the word or phrase appears in the document, e.g. see page 14.

1. Open the **Activity** document

2. Highlight the word "physical" in the second paragraph

3. On the **References tab** in the **Index** group, click on **Mark Entry**

4. Type in "exercise" for **Subentry**

5. Check the **Italic** checkbox

6. Click on **Mark All**

7. In the **Index** group, select **Insert Index**

8. Highlight the word "aerobics."

9. Click on **Mark Entry** in the **Index** group

10. Under **Options,** click on **Cross-reference**

11. After **See,** type in "exercise."

12. Click on the **Mark** button

13. Insert a **Page Break** at the end of the document

14. Type the heading "Index"

15. In the **Index** group, select **Insert Index**

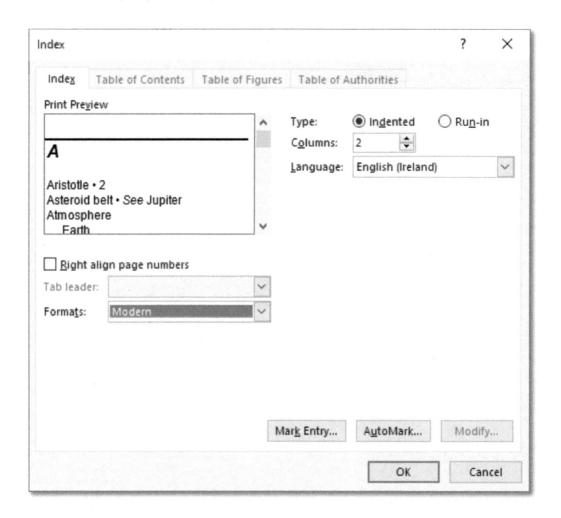

16. In **Formats,** choose **Modern**

17. Click **OK**

18. An index at the end of the document has been created

19. Insert a **Page Break** after the second paragraph

20. Locate the **Index** marked **Physical**

21. Highlight the **XE** index marking in the document

22. Click on **Delete**

23. This index has been removed from the document

24. Right-click on the index and select **Update Field** to update the index entries

25. Save the document as **Index**

Bookmarks

Bookmarks are used to mark positions in the text that may be important. For example, a subheading can be bookmarked and cross-referenced to show the reader where it appears in the document. Cross-references can be created with other references such as footnotes or endnotes.

1. Open the document **Physical benefits of walking**

2. Place your cursor before the "Walking" subheading

3. On the **Insert** tab in the **Links** group, click on **Bookmark**

4. Type in "Walking" for the **Bookmark Name**

5. Click on the **Add** button

6. A bookmark has been created

7. On the **Insert** tab, select **Links**, click on **Bookmark**

8. Select the "Walking" bookmark

9. Click on the **Delete** button

10. Select **Close**

11. The bookmark has been deleted

12. Save the document as **Bookmark**

Cross-Reference

A cross-reference is information provided to show where further details can be found on a topic, e.g. see page 3. This is useful for readers who want to find additional information about a topic covered. Cross-references can be applied to captions, footnotes, and endnotes. This can make finding information within a document more accessible.

1. Open the document **Aerobic Exercise**

2. Place the cursor at the start of the second page after the text "See page"

3. On the **References** tab in the **Captions** group, click on **Cross-Reference**

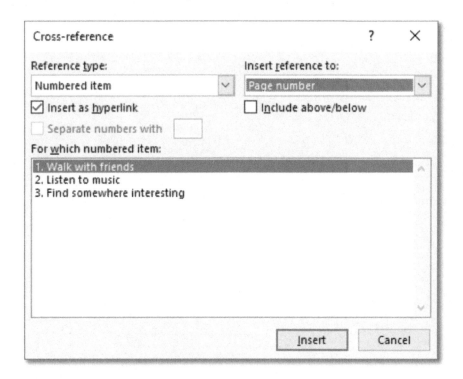

4. For **Reference Type,** select **Numbered Item**

5. For **Insert Reference To** select **Page Number**

6. Select the **Insert As Hyperlink** checkbox

7. For **Reference Type,** select **Numbered Item**

8. For **Insert Reference To** select **Paragraph Number**

9. Select the **Insert As Hyperlink** checkbox

10. Choose the "Increase Appetite" numbered item

11. Click on **Insert**

12. A cross-reference has been created

13. Choose the "Improve Sleep" numbered item

14. Click on **Insert**

15. Choose the "Help you lose weight" numbered item

16. Click on **Insert**

17. Hold down the **Ctrl** key and click on the cross-reference

18. You will be brought to the numbered item

19. On the **References** tab, click on **Cross-Reference**

20. For **Reference Type,** select **Heading**

21. For **Insert Reference to** choose **Heading Text**

22. Insert a **Cross-Reference** after "For information about Aerobic Exercise, see page"

23. Choose the **Aerobic Exercise** heading

24. Click on **Insert**

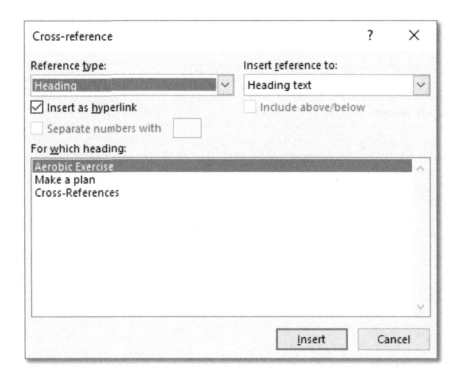

25. Insert a **Bookmark** called **Image** for the photograph on the first page of the document

26. On the **References** tab in the **Captions** group, select **Cross-Reference**

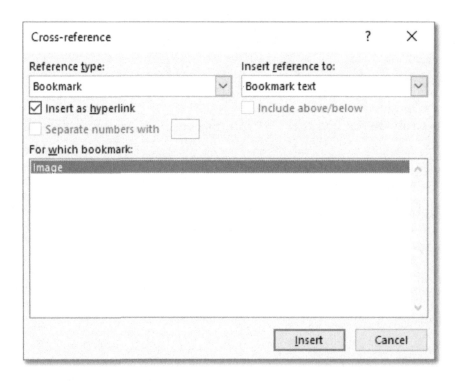

27. For **Reference Type,** choose **Bookmark**

28. Select the **Image** for the cross-reference

29. Click on **Insert**

30. On the **References** tab, click on **Cross-Reference**

31. For **Reference Type,** select **Table**

32. For **Insert Reference To** select **Entire Caption**

33. Select the **Insert As Hyperlink** checkbox

34. Choose **Table 1** as the object to be cross-referenced

35. Click on **Insert**

36. Save the document as **Cross Reference**

Fields

Fields provide a shortcut to inserting relevant information into a document. Fields are used to insert details into a document, such as author information, comments, the file size, or the subject. Information such as this can be included in the header or footer of a document. For example, you may want to have the document file name in the footer. This can be achieved by inserting the file name field into the footer.

1. Open the **Cross Reference** document

2. Double click at the top of the page to enter information into the header

3. Locate the **Insert** tab in the **Text** group

4. Click on **Explore Quick Parts** and choose **Fields**

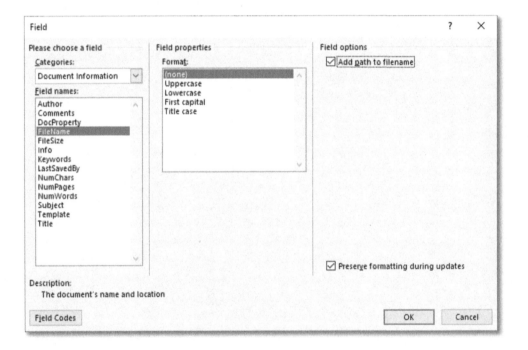

5. Under **Categories**, select **Document Information**

6. Under **Field Names**, choose **File Name**

7. Click **OK**

File Size

1. Place the cursor in the middle of the header

2. On the **Insert** tab in the **Text** group, select **Insert a Field**

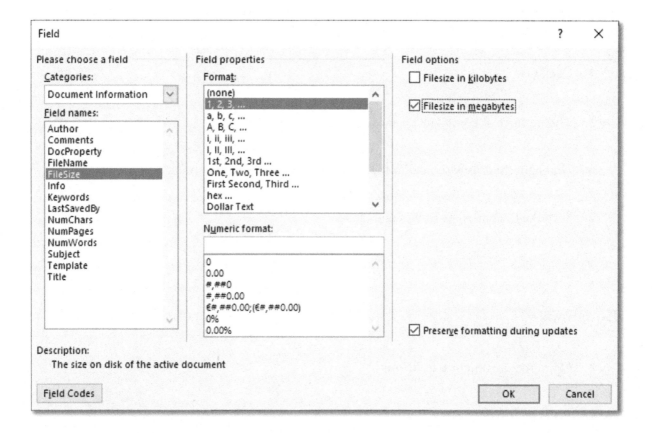

3. Under **Field Names,** choose **File Size**

4. Under **Field Options,** click on the **Filesize in Megabytes** checkbox

5. Click **OK**

6. Click **OK** again

7. The size of the file is displayed in megabytes

Number of Pages

1. Place the cursor in the centre of the footer

2. On the **Insert** tab in the **Text** group, select **Insert a Field**

3. Under **Field Names,** choose **NumPages**

4. Click **OK**

5. The number of pages will be shown in the footer

6. Highlight the **FileSize** field in the header and press the **Backspace** key to delete it

7. Save the document as **Fields** and close it

Equations

1. Open the document **Equations**

2. Place your cursor in the **January Total** cell

3. Open the **Fields** dialog box

4. Under **Categories,** choose **Equations and Formulas**

5. Under **Field Names,** click on = (Formula)

6. Click on the **Formulas…** button

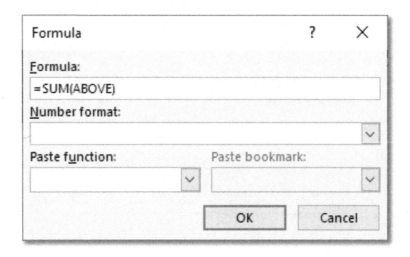

7. Enter =SUM(ABOVE)

8. This will add Sales and Marketing costs in January

9. Click **OK**

10. The total sales for January are calculated

11. Use the same equation to add February and March totals

12. Place the cursor in the **Average Expenses** cell in the following table

13. Open the **Fields** dialog box

14. Under **Categories,** choose **Equations and Formulas**

15. Under **Field Names,** click on = (Formula)

16. Click on the **Formulas...** button

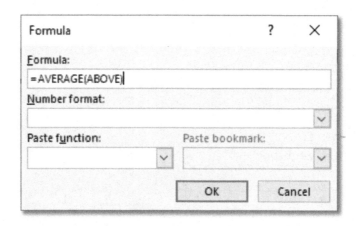

17. In the **Formula** textbox, **enter** =AVERAGE(ABOVE)

18. Click **OK**

19. Place the cursor in the **Count** answer cell in the **Employees** table

20. Open the **Fields** dialog box

21. Under **Categories,** choose **Equations and Formulas**

22. Under **Field Names,** click on = (Formula)

23. Click on the **Formulas…** button

24. Enter the **Formula** =COUNT(ABOVE)

25. Click **OK**

26. This has counted the number of employees in the table

27. Save the document as **Calculated**

Change a Field Number

The format of fields can be changed in a document. This may be applied to date fields where a different format needs to be displayed, e.g. dd mmm yy for 04 June 20.

1. Open the **Calculated** document

2. Open the **Field** dialog box

3. Click on the **Formula** button

4. Under **Number Format,** select the **Currency** format

5. Click **OK**

6. This has changed the format of the numbered fields

7. Double click on the header of the document

8. On the **Insert** tab in the **Text** group, click on **Quick Parts** and choose **Fields**

9. Under **Category,** choose **Date and Time**

10. Under **Field Name,** select **Date**

11. Under **Format,** choose the format **dd MMMM yyyy**

12. Click **OK**

13. This has inserted today's date into the document

14. Save the document and keep it open

Lock & Unlock Fields

Fields in a document can be locked to ensure that no changes are made. This is useful when creating forms in a document where you may want some fields to remain unchanged. Fields can also be unlocked when you need to edit a document. For example, you may want to create a form in a document for other people to fill out. By locking specific fields, labels will remain unchanged when other people fill out the document.

1. Open the **Equations** document

2. Double click on the header

3. On the **Insert** tab, click on **Insert a Field**

4. Under **Category,** choose **Date and Time**

5. Under **Date Formats,** select hh:mm:ss and click **OK**

6. This has inserted the current time into the document

7. Press **F9** to update the field

8. The time will be updated

9. Select the field and press **Ctrl+F11**

10. When you try to update the field, it remains the same

11. Unlock the field by selecting it and pressing **Ctrl+Shift+F11**

12. Press **F9** to update the field

13. The time has been updated

14. Save the document

Create a Form

Forms can be created in a document allowing other users to fill in details. You can use different fields, such as checkboxes, text fields, and drop-down menus of a form can provide other users with a means to enter personal details. For example, a club owner can create a form for members to fill in. The form can be adjusted so that recipients can only enter details in the spaces provided.

1. Open a new document

2. On the **File** tab, select **Options**

3. Select **Customize Ribbon**

4. In the list of **Main Tabs,** check **Developer**

5. Click on the **Add** button

6. Click **OK**

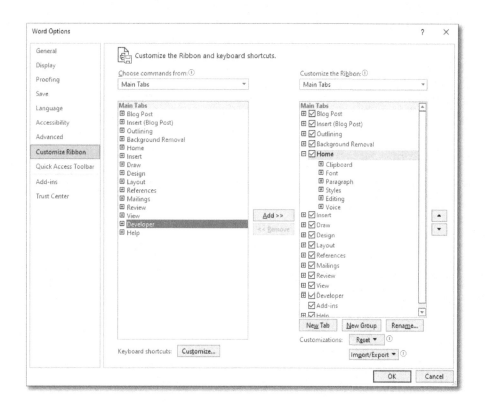

7. Type out the following form:

Personal Details

Name:

Are you a member?   Yes   No

Course:

8. On the **Developer** tab, click on **Legacy Tools** and select **Text Form Field**

9. A text field is entered into the form

10. After the Yes, Insert a **Check Box Form Field**

11. After the No, Insert another **Check Box Form Field**

12. After Course, insert **Combo Box**

13. Double click on the **Combo Box** field

14. In the **Drop-Down Item** text box, type in "Word."

15. Click the **Add** button

16. Type in "Excel" "PowerPoint" and "Access"

17. Include these as **Items in the drop-down list**

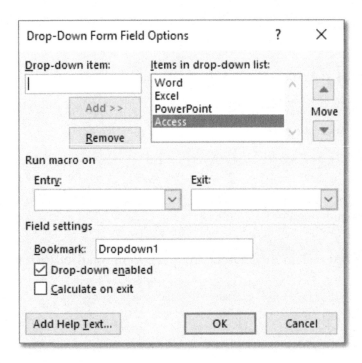

18. Click **OK**

19. Save the document as **Forms**

Protecting Forms

Forms can be protected so certain parts of the form cannot be changed, e.g. the first name label. This is useful if you want other people to fill in forms without changing the form itself. Only users with the password may edit the form.

1. Open the **Form** document

2. On the **Developer** tab in the **Protect** group, click on **Restrict Editing**

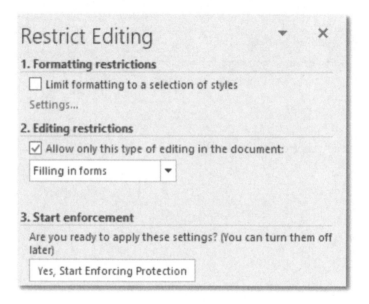

3. Under **Editing Restrictions, the second option**, select the **Allow Only This Type of Editing in the Document** checkbox

4. In the drop-down menu beneath, choose **Filling in Forms**

5. Click on the **Yes, Start Enforcing Protection** button

6. Enter in a password of **Pass** and **Re-enter** it to confirm

7. Click **OK**

8. Fill in your details in the form

9. When you have completed the form, click on **Stop Protection**

10. Enter in the password **Pass**

11. **Click** OK

12. The document is now ready to be edited

13. Enter a heading above the form **Membership Form**

14. On the **Developer** tab in the **Protect** group, click on **Restrict Editing**

15. Beneath **Editing Restrictions,** click on the **Allow Only This Type of Editing in the Document** checkbox

16. In the drop-down menu beneath, choose **No Changes (Read-Only)**

17. Click on the **Yes, Start Enforcing Protection** button

18. Enter in a password of **Protect** and **Re-enter** it to confirm

19. Click **OK**

20. Users can only view the form without being able to fill in details

21. Save the document as **Protected**

Save & Modify a Template

Templates can be used repeatedly and modified according to your needs. They are helpful for frequently carried out tasks, such as creating invoices or letters. Having a set template means that the same structured document can be used repeatedly. A template can also be modified, so they can be made to change the template's appearance if any changes are required.

1. Open the **Form** document

2. On the **File** tab, select **Save As Template**

3. Name the template "Club Membership."

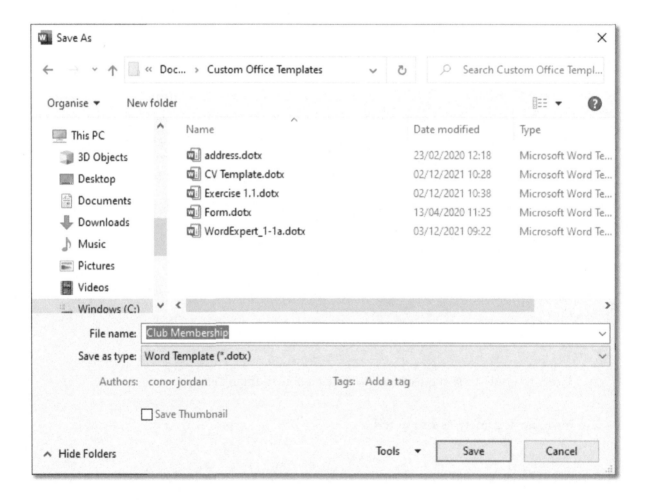

4. Click **Save** and close the document

5. On the **File** tab, select **Open** and click **Browse**

6. In the **Open** dialog box, find the **Custom Office Templates** folder

7. Select the **Form** template and click **Open**

8. Change the title of the form to "Course Registration Details."

9. Change the **Font** of the form to **Veranda**

10. **Save** and **Close** the document

11. The template has now been modified

12. Save the document and close it

Revision - Section 3

1. Open the document **Music**

2. Insert a **Caption** with the text "Guitar."

3. Delete the caption

4. Include a **Table Caption** above the table with the text "Music Sales."

5. Use a **Formula** to calculate the January column

6. Change the **Caption Numbering** to the format, i, ii, iii, ...

7. Insert a **Footnote** for the word "guitars" with the text "Musical Instrument."

8. Insert an **Endnote** for the word "nationwide" with the text "We will deliver throughout the country.'"

9. After the sentence "underrepresented localities" insert a **Citation** with the following information:

   • Title: National Report on Economy

   • Publisher: The Government

   • Year: 2021

   • Author: Ms Joan Smith, Mr Mark Hughes, Mrs Henrietta Juliet

10. Include a **Bibliography** after the body of text in the document

11. Save the document as **Music Edited**

12. Open the document **Contents**

13. Format the subheadings using **Styles**

14. Insert a **Table of Contents**

15. Insert a **Caption** of **Figure** for each of the pictures

16. Insert a **Table of Figures** at the beginning of the document

17. Highlight the word "Food" in the third paragraph

18. Mark all and create an **Index** for it at the end of the document

19. Create a **Bookmark** for each subheading

20. **Cross Reference** the word "dehydrated'" in the second paragraph

21. Include the subheading "Cut Down on Caffeine."

22. Insert the **FileName** in the footer using **Fields**

23. Lock the **FileName** field

24. Save the document as **Healthy Eating**

25. Create a **Form** with a text field for **Name** and a **Checkbox** for **Gender**

26. **Protect the Form** using a password

27. Save the form as a template named **Revised**

Summary

Referencing

In this section, you have learned how to:

- Insert citations, bibliographies, tables of contents and figures
- Create forms using fields such as text fields and check boxes
- Restrict editing using password protection for form filling and read-only purposes

Section 4

Mail Merge

In this section, you will learn how to:

- Create and modify data sources
- Produce customised letters for recipients
- Use advanced mail merge features

Creating a Data Source

When sending out letters to many people, it is important to have contact details such as first name, address line, telephone number and email. These pieces of information are fields and can be included in letters. When creating a data source, these details will post similar letters to recipients with different addresses. This is why creating an accurate data source is essential.

For example, when a retail company wants to send out the same letter containing an offer for their range of new products, they can create a data source containing fields with customer details. These fields can then be included as the address on each personalised letter and sent out to the company's customers.

1. Open a blank document

2. On the **Mailings** tab, click on **Select Recipients** and **Type a New List**

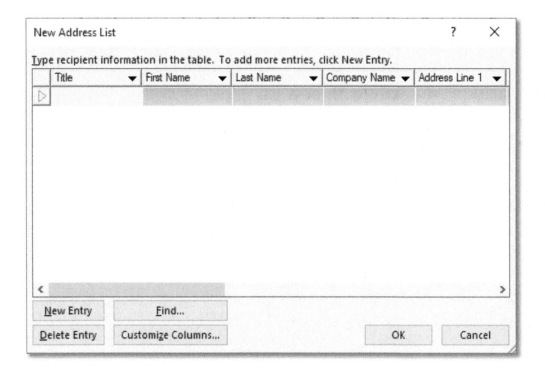

3. Click on **Customize Address List**

4. Rename the **City** label with **Town** and **Last Name** with **Surname**

5. Rename **Address Line 1** as **Address1** and **Address Line 2** as **Address2**

6. Organise the list with the following headings

7. **First Name**, **Surname**, **Address1**, **Address2,** and **Town**

8. Click **OK**

9. Enter the following list of contact details into your fields

10. Use the **Tab** key to move on to the next entry:

First Name: Mary, John, James, Henry, Sarah

Last Name: Jones, Murphy, Smith, Hughes, Nolan

Address1:   Main Street, Riverside, Townview, Main Street, Riverview

Address2:   Everglade, Tree Grove, River Avenue, Everglade, Grove

Town: Cityview, Townside, Main Town, Cityview, Townside

11. Click **OK** and save the data source as **Contact List**

Editing a Data Source

Existing data sources can be edited if details change, e.g. a customer changes address or contact number. This does not change the letters that recipients will receive. It will change the contact details of the letter recipients. For example, when a computer company wants to send out a discount to customers, but some have moved to another address, this can be updated by editing the company's data source.

1. With the blank document open, click on **Edit Recipient List**

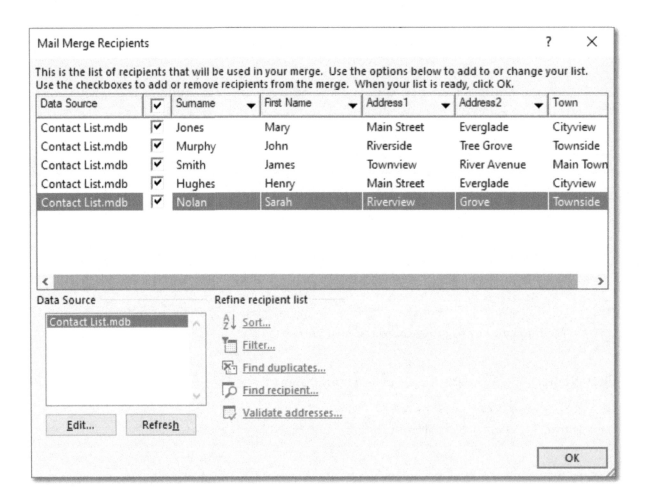

2. Select the **Data Source Contact List** and click **Edit**

3. Click on the **New Entry** button

4. Add a new entry:

First Name:	John
Surname:	Brennan
Address1:	Sideview
Address2:	Glenpark
Town:	Cityscape

5. Select the Henry Hughes entry

6. Click on **Delete Entry**

7. Click **Yes**

8. Click **OK** and select **Yes** when prompted

9. Under **Refine Recipient List,** select **Sort**

10. Choose to sort by **Surname Ascending**

11. Click **OK**

12. Under **Refine Recipient List,** select **Filter**

13. Select the **Filter Records** tab

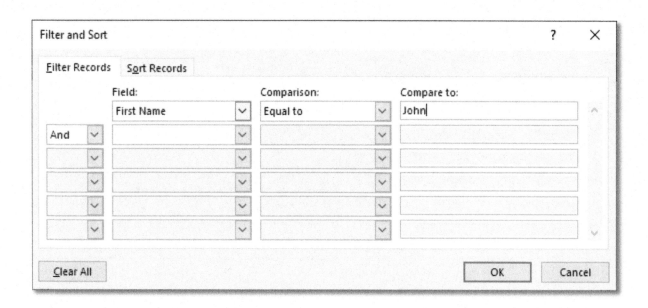

14. Choose to sort **First Name Equal** to "John."

15. Choose **First Name** as the **Field** and **Comparison** as **Is Not Blank**

16. Click **OK**

17. Save the document

Ask Field

Ask Fields are used in a mail merge document to display a dialog box each time you merge a data record. When a user creates letters, a dialog box will appear, prompting the user to enter information. This can act as a helpful reminder when preparing letters to send to recipients.

For example, when sending out letters to customers that require today's date, Word can prompt you to enter the correct date before merging the data record and sending out the letters to customers. Reminders to enter the correct information for fields such as Telephone Number or Email Address for customers can be set up using ask fields. This reduces the risk of errors occurring when sending out letters.

1. Open the blank document

2. On the **Mailings** tab, click on **Insert Merge Field**

3. Select the relevant field for the letter

4. Create the following document and insert merge fields

5. Click on the **Insert Merge Fields** button in the **Write & Insert Fields**:

22/11/2021

Computer Store

«FirstName»

«Surname»

«Address1»

«Address2»

«Town»

Dear «FirstName» «Surname»,

As one of our valued customers, we are delighted to inform you that you are eligible for a   %
discount on our range of laptops and electronic devices.

George Smith

Computer Store Manager

6. Highlight the **Date** at the beginning of the document

7. Insert a **Bookmark** called **Date** and select **Add**

8. On the **Mailings** tab, click on **Rules** and choose **Ask**

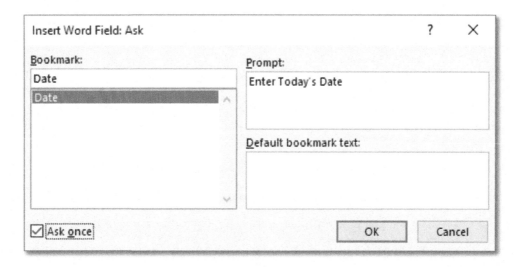

9. Select the bookmark **Date**

10. Enter "Enter Today's Date" in the Prompt text box.

11. Click **OK**

12. Select the checkbox **Ask Once**

13. Click **OK**

14. You will be prompted to enter today's date

15. Enter today's date and click **OK**

16. Save the document as **Computer Offer**

If Then Else Fields

If then else fields can be included in a mail merge document to produce different letters for different people. For example, if the recipient has been with the company for over a year, they can receive a letter with a discount. People who have not been with the company for a year will receive a letter with a lower discount.

This feature is used to send letters containing different information based on who will be receiving the letter. **If** a field name is equal to a particular name, e.g. customer name, **Then** another field will contain a value, e.g. a discount, **Else** another field will have a different value, e.g. a lower discount.

1. Using the **Computer Offer** document and the same data source

2. Display the **Mailings** tab

3. Place the cursor to the left of the percentage sign

4. Click on **Rules** and choose **If...Then...Else**

5. Enter the information provided below:

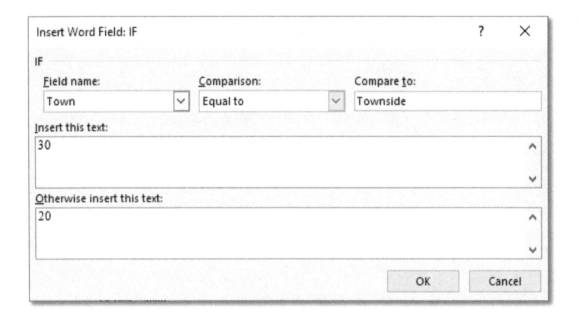

6. Click **OK**

7. This will display 30% for people living in Townside and 20% for everybody else

8. Save the document but leave it open

Merging

This is the final step in the mail merge process. The letters are created and prepared to be sent out to recipients. It is important to go through each step slowly to ensure that details are accurate and that the letters are prepared correctly.

Merging involves combining all the information in the data sources with the letters to be sent out. For example, a company will want to include all the addresses and contact details in each letter by merging the data source with the letters created.

1. Open the **Computer Offer** document

2. On the **Mailings** tab, select **Finish & Merge**

3. Choose **Edit Individual Documents**

4. Individual letters have been created for each customer

5. There will be two letters created

6. Different discounts are offered to customers named John

7. Save the letters as **Sent letters**

Revision - Section 4

1. Open a **New Document**

2. Create a **Data Source** with the following information:

First Name

John	Mary	George

Surname

Smith	Watson	Jones

Address1

Newtown	Main Street	Glenview

Town

Atlantis	Newville	Old Town

3. Save the data source as **Client List**

4. **Edit** the data source by including the following record:

First Name	Surname	Address Line 1	Town
Sarah	Walsh	Main Street	Newville

5. **Sort the Records** by surname ascending

6. Type out the following letter and insert **Merge Fields**:

3/11/20

«First_Name»

«Surname»

«Address1»

«Town»

Dear «First_Name» «Surname»,

As a valued customer, you have been entered into a prize draw for €. We hope that you remain a loyal user of our services.

Kind regards

James Mathews

7. Add a **Bookmark** to the date

8. Use the **Ask** function to prompt users to enter today's date

9. Use the **If...Then...Else** function to insert €2,000 if the Town field is equal to Newville; otherwise, insert €1,000

10. Create the letters for the recipients

11. Save the letter as **Prize**

Summary
Mail Merge

In this section, you have learned how to:

- Create and edit data sources from contact and address lists
- Include Ask fields to prompt mail merge users and If…Then…Else… fields for customised letters
- Merge letters for delivery to recipients

Section 5

Linking

In this section, you will learn how to:

- Create external links to documents
- Embed objects without links
- Edit and remove links between files

Linking & Embedding

Links can be placed in a document linking them to other documents or files. When you make a change in the original document, this is reflected in the linked document. Embedding an object means placing an object in a document without a link. When you make a change in the original document, there is no change reflected in the embedded document.

1. Open a **New Document**

2. On the **Insert** tab in the **Illustrations** group, click on the **Chart** button and choose a **Pie Chart**

3. Fill in the following details:

Annual	**Sales**
1st Qtr	€23,500
2nd Qtr	€32,500
3rd Qtr	€18,500
4th Qtr	€15,500

4. On the **Insert** tab in the **Text** group, click on the **Object** button

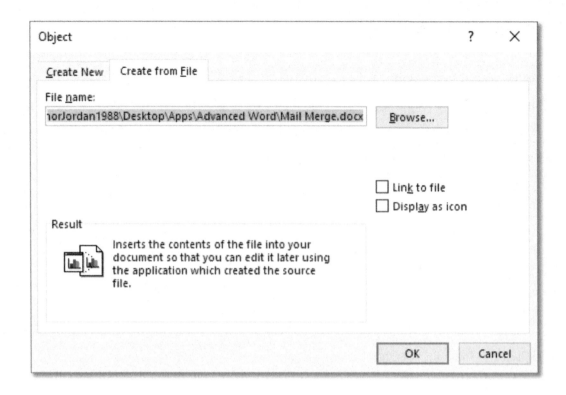

5. Select **Microsoft Word Document**

6. Select the **Create From File** tab

7. Select the **Display as Icon** checkbox

8. Navigate to your exercises folder and select the **Computer Offer** document

9. The embedded text will appear in the document beneath the pie chart

10. Save the document as **Linked**

11. On the **Insert** tab, select **Link** and click on **Insert Link**

12. Select the **Web Page or File** tab

13. Click on **Select** and choose the **Linked** document

14. Make a change to the header of the **Computer Offer** document and save it

15. Re-open the **Linked** document

16. Select **Yes** in the dialog box

17. On the **Insert** tab, in the **Text** group, click on the arrow beside **Object**

18. Choose **Text From File**

19. Select the **Letter Document**

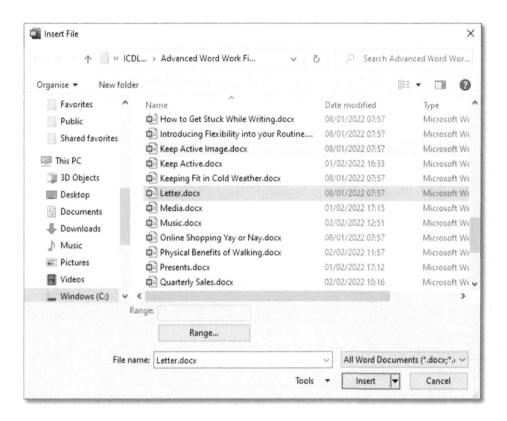

20. Next to the **Insert** button, click on the **Arrow** and select **Insert as Link**

21. Include a heading in the document titled "Letter" and save it

22. The changes will be updated in the linked document

23. Save the document

Display as Icon

1. Open the **Linked** document

2. On the **Insert** tab, click on the **Object** button

3. Click on the **Create From File** tab

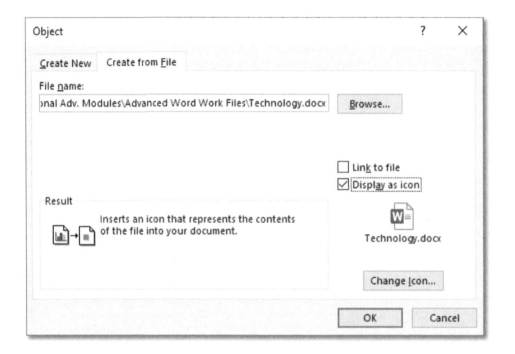

4. Select **Browse**

5. Click on **From File** and choose the **Technology** document

6. Select the **Display as Icon** checkbox

7. Click **OK**

8. The object will be displayed as an icon in the document

9. Save the document as **Display as Icon**

Break a Link

Links between documents and files can be broken when there is no longer a need for a link. This means that changes to an original file will not be reflected in the unlinked document. For example, the link can be removed when you no longer need a link between a budget in a spreadsheet and a report document. Any changes in the document will not be shown in the spreadsheet either.

1. Open the **Display as Icon** document

2. Right-click on the **Technology** word document icon

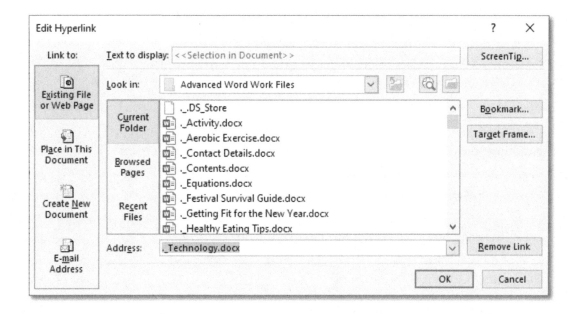

3. Click on **Remove Link**

4. Click **OK**

5. Both documents are unlinked

6. Save the document as **Broken Link**

Embedding Data

When you place an object in a document, it can be embedded without creating a link. This means that the object placed in the document can only be changed in that document and not any other document. There is no link between the object and any additional file. For example, a pie chart embedded in a document cannot be changed by another file, such as a spreadsheet.

1. Open a **New Document**

2. On the **Insert** tab, click on **Object**

3. Choose **Microsoft Excel Chart** on the **Create From File** tab

4. Navigate to the exercises folder and select the **Pie Chart** spreadsheet

5. Click **OK**

6. Rearrange the chart and data table so that they fit within the document

7. Save the document as **Embedded**

8. Select the chart and press **Delete** to remove the object

9. Close the document without saving

Revision - Section 5

1. Create a **Blank Document**

2. Insert the Save Money on Holidays document as an object

3. Create a **Link** to the document

4. Save the document as **Linked**

5. Change the **Font** in the document to **Arial**

6. Notice the effect this has on the **Linked** document

7. Break the link between the external document

8. Save the document as **Revision 5** and close it

Summary

Linking

In this section, you have learned how to:

- Link text, URLs, images, and charts to external files
- Embed text and pictures without links into documents
- Modify and delete links to other files

Section 6

Automation

In this section, you will learn how to:

- Create and edit macros for automated tasks
- Apply automatic text production and correction settings
- Adjust automated formatting in documents

AutoFormat

AutoFormat formats an entire document using a pre-set style. Formatting in this way applies a consistent style to the document. It is an efficient way of maintaining a similar style throughout a document.

1. Open the **Reduce your carbon footprint** document

2. Click on the **Customize Quick Access Toolbar** arrow

3. Choose **More Commands**

4. Under **Choose Commands From** select **All Commands**

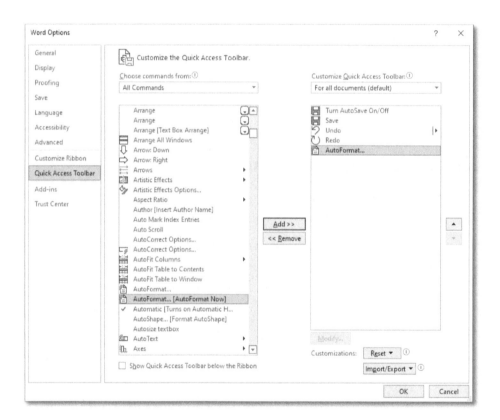

5. Scroll down until you find **AutoFormat**

6. Click on the **Add** button and click **OK**

7. Click on the **AutoFormat** button

8. Click **OK**

9. A formatting style has been applied to the document

10. Save the document as **Formatted**

11. Leave the document open

AutoCorrect

AutoCorrect allows you to input words to replace other selected words. For instance, if you want your initials to display your name automatically, these settings can be applied to your document. When you type in your initials, your name will appear. It is helpful to enter long, complicated words into a document frequently and want to use an abbreviation that displays the entire word.

For example, suppose you enter complex words into documents regularly. In that case, AutoCorrect can efficiently enter these details into your document.

1. Open the **Formatted** document

2. Open **Preferences** and select **AutoCorrect**

3. On the **File** tab, choose **Options**

4. Select **Proofing** and click on the **AutoCorrect Options** button

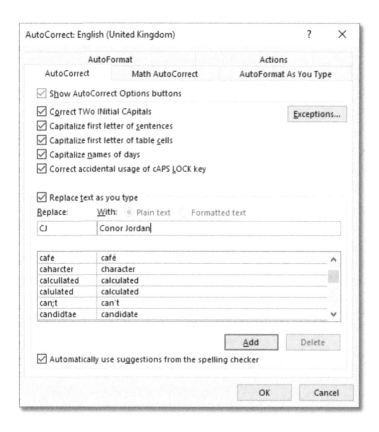

5. With the **AutoCorrect** tab selected, type in your initials into the **Replace** text box and in the **With** text box, type your name

6. Click **OK**

7. Place your cursor at the end of the document and type in your initials

8. Your full name will appear

9. Open the **AutoCorrect** dialog box again and locate the entry you created

10. Change the initials with the text **ICDL** and choose to replace it with **International Computer Driving License**

11. Click **OK**

12. Enter in the text **ICDL** at the end of the document

13. Open the **AutoCorrect** dialog box again and locate the entry you created

14. Click on the **Delete** button

15. This deletes the **AutoCorrect** entry

16. Click **OK**

17. Save the document as **Autocorrect**

AutoText

AutoText is used for frequently used text, such as addresses or names. This is useful when repeating tasks often, e.g. when creating letters. The AutoText entry can be prepared by entering its name, category, and description.

1. Open the **Letters** document

2. Highlight the name and address at the top of the letter

3. On the **Insert** tab in the **Text** group, hover over **Explore Quick Parts**

4. Select **AutoText,** then choose **Save Selection to AutoText Gallery**

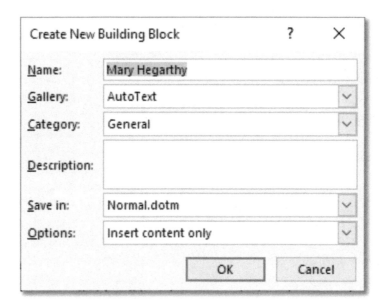

5. Click **OK**

6. This address will be available to include in other documents

7. Save the document as **Autotext**

Modify an AutoText Entry

The contents of AutoText entries can be modified so that different text appears when specific initials, acronyms or abbreviations are input into a document. For example, when entering tm into a document, this can be modified from Trade Mark to Trademark. AutoText entries can be deleted when they are no longer required.

1. Open the **Auto text** document

2. On the **Insert** tab in the **Text** group, click on **Explore Quick Parts**

3. Select **Building Blocks Organizer**

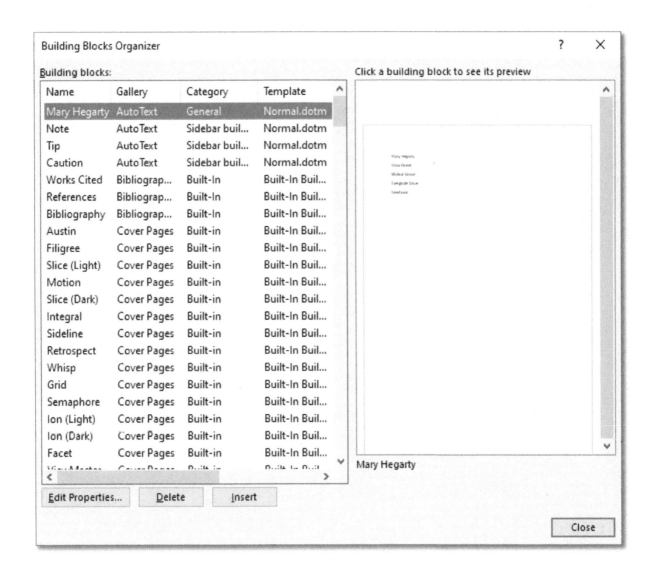

4. Select the **AutoText** entry beginning with **Mary**

5. Click on **Edit Properties**

6. Change the surname to **Dunne**

7. Click **Yes**

8. Open a new document

9. Begin typing Mary

10. The address will appear

11. Click **Enter** to fill in the address

12. Save the document as **Address Edited**

13. Open **Preferences** and select **AutoText**

14. Locate the address and click on **Delete**

15. The AutoText entry has now been deleted. Save the document

Create a Macro

A macro is an automatic function that carries out several tasks when run. This is useful when a task needs to be repeated many times and can save time by formatting, adjusting paragraphs, or changing styles. When a macro is set up, the user can simply click on a button, and the set of instructions are carried out instantly.

1. Open a **New Document**

2. On the **Developer** tab in the **Code** group, click on **Record Macro**

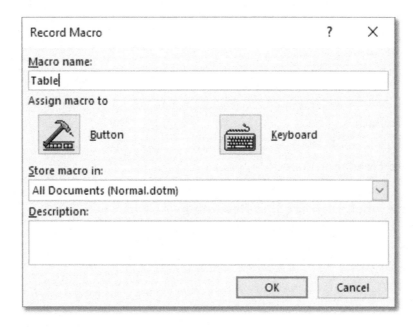

3. Name the **Macro** as "Table" and click **OK**

4. On the **Insert** tab in the **Tables** group, create a table with four columns and three rows

5. Format the table as **Grid Table 4 – Accent 6**

6. On the **Table Tools Layout** tab in the **Data** group, select **Repeat Header Rows**

7. On the **Developer** tab in the **Code** group, choose **Stop Recording**

8. On the **Developer** tab, click on **Record Macro**

9. Name the **Macro** as "Print_Page" and click **OK**

10. On the **Layout** tab, select **Margins** and adjust the **Top, Right & Left** margins to 2.5cm and the **Bottom** margin to 3cm in **Custom Margins**

11. Click **OK**

12. On the **Insert** tab, click on **Header** and select **Edit Header**

13. Select **Field** and choose **Document Information**

14. Choose **File Name** and click **OK**

15. On the **Insert** tab and find the **Header & Footer** group, click on **Footer**

16. Select **Edit Footer**

17. **On the Header & Footer** group in the **Insert** group, select **Document Info**

18. Choose **File Path**

19. Select **Close Header & Footer**

20. On the **Developer** tab, select **Stop Recording**

21. Save the document as **Macro**

Run a Macro

A macro is run to perform its recorded tasks. Each recorded step will be carried out again when the macro is run.

1. Open the **Macro** document

2. On the **Developer** tab, select **Macros**

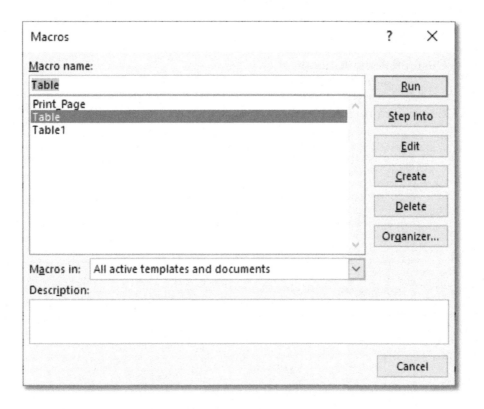

3. Select **Table** and select **Run**

4. This button will run the macro, and the formatted table will appear

5. On the **Developer** tab, select **Macros**

6. Select "Print_Page" and click on **Run**

7. This will run the macro and adjust page setup settings

8. Close the document without saving

Creating a Custom Button

A custom button for a macro can be created to identify it on the ribbon. The macro runs when you click on the button, and all the recorded tasks are repeated. A custom button can be created that identifies the macro.

1. Open the **Macro** document

2. Right-click on a space on the ribbon

3. Choose **Customize the Ribbon**

4. In the **Choose Commands From** drop-down box, choose **Macros**

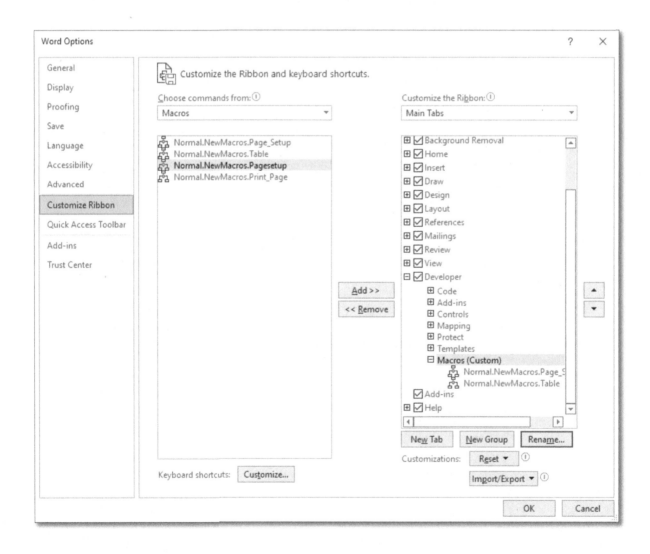

5. Click on the **New Group** button to create a new group

6. Click on the **Rename** button

7. Change the name of the group to **Macros**

8. Click **OK**

9. Select both the **Table** and the **Page_Setup** macros and click on the **Add** button

10. Click on the **Right-Hand Arrow** button to add both macros to the group

11. Click on the **Rename** button

12. Choose an **Exclamation Mark** for the icon

13. Change the **Display Name** to **Table**

14. Click on the **Rename** button

15. Choose a **Smiley Face** for the icon

16. Change the **Display Name** to **Page_Setup**

17. Click **Save**

18. The **Macro** is now added to the **Ribbon**

19. Save the document

Revision - Section 6

1. Open the **Letter** document

2. Use **AutoFormat** to format the entire document

3. Using **AutoCorrect**, replace your initials with your full name

4. Type out your initials to enter your name above the address

5. Delete the **AutoCorrect** information

6. Highlight the name and address and use **AutoText** to save the selection to the **AutoText** gallery

7. Modify the **AutoText** entry by inserting your name

8. Delete the **AutoText** entry

9. Create a **Macro** that formats the document in Arial 14pt Justified with 1.5 line spacing named "Format."

10. Choose an **Exclamation** Mark as a custom button for the macro

11. **Run** the Macro to see its effect

12. Save the document as **Automation**

Summary

Automation

In this section, you have learned how to:

- Record, run and customise macros

- Use AutoText and AutoCorrect features to adjust text

- Apply consistent formatting to documents using AutoFormat

Section 7

Editing

In this section, you will learn how to:

- Review documents and collaborate with other users
- Compare and combine revised documents
- Apply page layout settings and security

Tracking Changes

Changes can be tracked when reviewing a document to assess and review edited text by other users. This is useful when editing a document in collaboration with another person. This feature can show where changes in a document have been made or need to be reviewed. For example, when a manager reviews a report created by an employee, any changes made by the manager can be viewed and changed if necessary.

1. Open the document **Sources available to a journalist**

2. Save the document as **Revision1**

3. On the **Review** tab, click on **Track Changes** and choose **For Everyone**

4. Choose **All Markup**

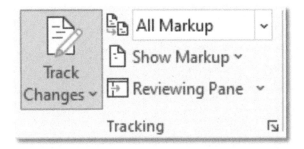

5. Delete the first sentence

6. At the end of the document, type: "For further information, visit your local library."

7. On the **Review** tab in the **Tracking** group, change **All Markup** to **Simple Markup**

8. Click on the bar beside the paragraph to redisplay the **Detailed Markup**

9. In the **Tracking** group, select **Show Markup** and select **Comments**

10. This will not display **Comments** in the document

11. In the **Tracking** group, select **Show Markup** and select **Balloons**

12. Select to **Show only Comments and Formatting in Balloons**

13. Only **Comments** added to the document and **Formatting** will be shown in balloons to the right of the document

14. On the **Review** tab, click on **Track Changes** and turn off **For Everyone**

15. Change **All Markup** to **No Markup**

16. On the **View** tab, select **Web Layout**

17. Save the document as **Revision 1**

Accept/Reject Changes

Depending on the requirements, any changes can be accepted or rejected when reviewing a document. This is a feature that can be used when collaborating on a project.

1. Open the **Revision 1** document

2. On the **Review** tab, click on **Accept-to-accept** changes made or **Reject** to decline the changes made to the document

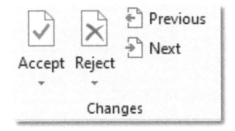

3. Highlight the second sentence beginning "Indirect quotations."

4. On the **Review** tab, select **New Comment**

5. Type in "These are not direct quotes from people"

6. Right-click on the location of the comment in the document and choose **Reply to Comment**

7. Type "They are paraphrased quotes"

8. Right-click on the location of the comment in the document and choose **Resolve Comment**

9. Highlight the second paragraph beginning "Journalists can research online articles."

10. On the **Review** tab, select **New Comment**

11. Type in "Make sure to check sources"

12. Click on **Show Comments** to reveal comments

13. Click on **Hide Comments** to hide comments from view

14. Return to the "They are paraphrased quotes" comment and edit it to read "They are quotes from people."

15. Select the comment in the second paragraph

16. On the **Review** tab, find the **Comments** group, click on **Delete**

17. This will remove the comment

18. Delete the first sentence in the third paragraph

19. Save the changed document as **Revision 2**

Compare and Combine Documents

Separate documents can be compared with each other. This is useful when comparing a revised document with its original. Differences in each document are highlighted, making editing easier. Word also allows you to combine documents while retaining any information contained within the original. This will keep the original document and include any changes made to the revised document. You can then accept and reject any necessary changes.

1. Open both the **Revision 1** and **Revision 2** document

2. On the **Review** tab, select **Compare,** then select **Combine**

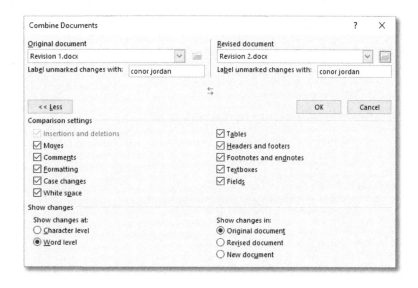

3. For **Original Document,** select **Revision 1**

4. For **Revised Document,** select **Revision 2**

5. Click **OK**

6. Accept all changes made to the document and save it as **Complete**

Password Protection

A document can be protected with a password, so only those with the password may change it. Formatting can be restricted so that people without a password may change certain parts of a document, e.g. when filling in a form. This is useful when you want to keep the contents of a document private and only share it with people who have the password.

1. Open the **Complete** document

2. On the **Review** tab, find the **Protect** group, click on **Restrict Editing**

3. Click on the **Limit Formatting to a selection of styles** checkbox

4. In the **Allow only this type of Editing in the Document** drop-down box, select **No Changes (Read-Only)**

5. Click on **Yes, Start Enforcing Protection**

6. Enter in a password of **Secret** twice and click **OK**

7. The document is now protected

8. Click on **Stop Protecting** in the **Restrict Editing** pane

9. Enter in your password and click **OK**

10. The document is now unprotected

11. Under **Editing Restrictions,** choose **Tracked Changes**

12. Click on **Yes, Start Enforcing Protection**

13. Tracked changes is the only editing that can be done in the document

14. Save the document as **Confidential**

Section Breaks

A section break is inserted when you want a space between one part of a document and another, e.g. having odd page titles such as chapter name on one page and section name on another displayed in the header of a book. Section breaks are often used when applied to headers and footers. Different formatting can be applied to other sections within the document with section breaks.

1. Open the **Completed** document

2. Place your cursor after the first header

3. On the **Layout** tab in the **Page Setup** group, click on **Breaks**

4. Choose **Even Page**

5. Place your cursor after the second paragraph

6. On the **Layout** tab, click on **Breaks**

7. Choose **Odd Page**

8. On the **Home** tab in the **Paragraph** group, click on the **Show/Hide** button

9. Place the cursor before the first section break and press the **Delete** key

10. Repeat the same task for the second section break

11. Save the document and leave it open

Page Setup

It is essential to prepare documents before printing to ensure they appear presentable. The layout, margins and type of paper used to print documents can be adjusted in the page setup dialog box. The size of headers and footers can be adjusted, and vertical alignment can be changed. This is an important step to complete before printing.

1. Open the **Completed** document

2. On the **Layout** tab, click on **Orientation**

3. Choose **Landscape**

4. Click on **File** and **Page Setup**

5. Select the **Layout** tab

6. Under **Page** change the **Vertical Alignment** to **Center**

7. Click **OK**

8. Save the document as **Page Setup**

Headers & Footers

Headers and footers can be formatted to change the first, odd and even pages. Page numbers, essay title, file size and document name can all be included in the header and footer of a document. It is essential to have relevant information related to the document in the header or footer.

1. Open the **Page Setup** document

2. On the **Insert** tab, click on **Header** and choose **Edit Header**

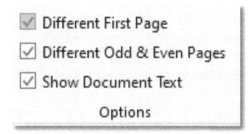

3. On the **Header & Footer** tab, select the **Different First Page** checkbox

4. Select the **Different Odd & Even Pages** checkbox

5. On the **Header & Footer** tab, select **Date & Time**

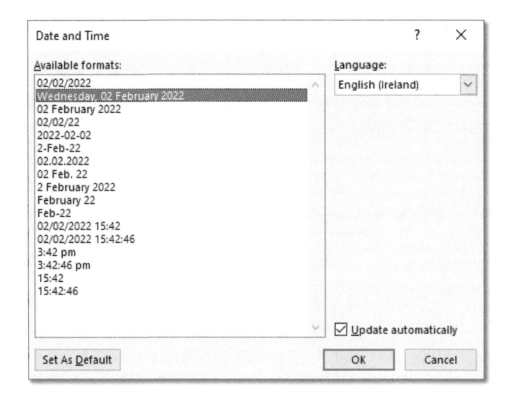

6. Select the above format and click **OK**

7. Click on **Go To Footer**

8. Select **Field** and choose **Document Info** and choose **FileName**

9. Click **OK**

10. Select the **Link to Previous** checkbox

11. This links the footer to the previous header

12. The link between header and footer can be removed by deselecting this checkbox

13. Save the document and leave it open

Watermark

A watermark is transparent text that appears in the background of a document. Different watermarks can be applied to documents, e.g. the word confidential to a document containing sensitive information. The colour of the watermark, its transparency, the font used, its size, and the layout of the watermark can be adjusted.

1. Open the **Page Setup** document

2. On the **Design** tab, find the **Page Background** group, select **Watermark**

3. Choose **Custom Watermark**

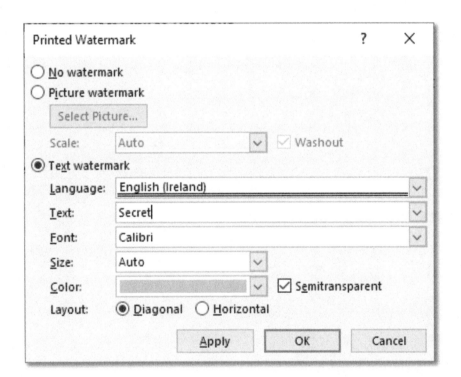

4. Choose **Text Watermark**

5. In the **Text** box, type in **Secret**

6. Click **OK**

7. The watermark is applied to the document

8. On the **Design** tab, find the **Page Background** group, click on **Watermark**

9. Choose **Remove Watermark**

10. Save the document

Spelling

The language used for spell-checking a document can be changed. This is useful when you want to check the spelling of a document in a foreign language. It is essential to spell-check a document before saving or printing.

1. Open the **Online Shopping Yay or Nay** document

2. On the **File** tab, click on **Options**

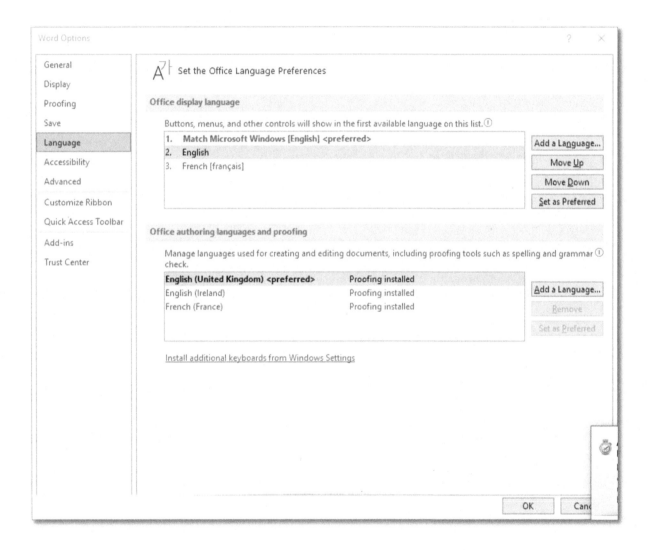

3. Select **Language**

4. Under **Office authoring languages and proofing, select the** Add a Language **button**

5. Choose **English (United Kingdom)** as the language and select **Add**

6. Click on the **Set as Preferred** button for **English (United Kingdom)** to make that the preferred language

7. On the **Review** tab, find the **Proofing** group, click on **Editor**

8. Double click on the **Spelling** label and review the document

9. Accept and reject changes as required

10. Save the document as **Checked**

Thesaurus

A thesaurus provides you with alternative words to a selected word. This is used when finding the right word to describe a sentence clearly. Rather than searching online or referring to a hard copy thesaurus, you can find alternative words using the built-in thesaurus in Word.

1. Highlight the word "Journalist" in the document

2. On the **Review** tab, find the **Proofing** group, and click on **Thesaurus**

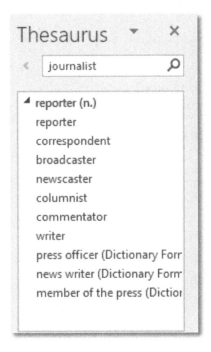

3. Choose the word "Journalist."

4. A list of synonyms will appear in a list on the **Thesaurus** pane

5. Select "Reporter"

6. The word will be replaced in the document

7. Save the document as **Revised**

Revision - Section 7

1. Open the **Technology** document

2. Turn on **Track Changes** and delete the first sentence

3. Change the tracking to **Simple Markup**

4. Add a new sentence after the first paragraph with the text:

    "Technology has improved all of our lives".

5. Save the document as **Technology 1**

6. **Accept All Changes** to the document

7. **Add a Comment** after this sentence with the text:" Needs some revision."

8. **Hide All Comments** in the document

9. Save the document as **Technology 2**

10. **Combine** both documents

11. Accept all changes to the document

12. Apply **Password Protection** to the document with the password "Secret."

13. Using section breaks, format the document so the page numbers only appear on odd pages

14. Apply a **Custom Margin** of 3cm for the Left and Right margins and 5cm for the Top and Bottom margins

15. Insert the Date & Time for the **Header**

16. Apply a **Custom Watermark** with the text "Confidential."

17. **Spell Check** the document

18. Use the **Thesaurus** to find different words for **Computer** and **Population** in the first paragraph

19. Save the document as **Fully Revised**

Summary

Editing

In this section, you have learned how to:

- Use the tracking changes editing features
- Compare and combine different versions of a document
- Apply page setup settings, including margins, orientation, layout and password security

Index

Printed in Great Britain
by Amazon

19758607R00099